Worthy of Worship

by

Sammy Tippit

MOODY PRESS
CHICAGO

All Scripture quotations, unless noted otherwise, are from the *New American Standard Bible,* © 1960, 1962, 1963, 1968, 1971, 1972, 1973, 1975, and 1977 by The Lockman Foundation, and are used by permission.

Library of Congress Cataloging in Publication Data

Tippit, Sammy.
    Worthy of worship / by Sammy Tippit.
        p.   cm.
    Includes bibliographies.
    ISBN 0-8024-9236-3
    1. God—Worship and love.   2. Worship.   3. Public worship.
    I. Title.
    BV4817.T56   1989
    291.3'8—dc20   89-32996

2 3 4 5 6 Printing/LC/Year 93 92 91

Printed in the United States of America

To those men who hold me accountable
in my Christian walk and ministry:
Frank Corte, Dr. Joe Ford, Chuck Hollimon, Jerry Jenkins,
Lt. Col. John Labash, Morris Todd, and Dr. David Walker

Contents

Foreword

I first "met" Sammy Tippit through the reading of his books *Fire in Your Heart* and *The Prayer Factor*. Immediately I felt that here was a young man I wanted to know. Though I had never actually met him, I sensed that his heart beat with mine in the matters of holiness of life, prayer, evangelism, discipleship, and the Great Commission.

Now I want you to "meet" Sammy and to sense for yourself his great heart for our Lord and the need to worship Him in more meaningful ways.

All Christians know in their heart of hearts that they need to worship God. But today, for so many, worship seems to be a lost art, no longer essential to our Sunday morning services or our personal devotions. It is too easy to go through the motions—or to neglect worship entirely—while our minds race on to other things. We like to be entertained, even in church. So, while we know that we should probably be more serious about focusing our attention on God and His attributes, we tend to forget the centrality of worship, both personal and corporate, in our faith.

Even when we acknowledge the necessity for worship, most Christians admit that they do not know exactly *how* to worship God—what to do and what to say. Should we stand or sit, shout or be still, express emotion or remain stoic? Sometimes we even argue about what form is proper.

This book directs us to the only Object of worship who is truly worthy: God Himself. Instead of focusing on ourselves or on our fellow man, we can focus fully on Him because His character merits our unquestioning adoration.

Only God can fulfill the deep longing within man to recognize Someone as complete purity and holiness.

Worthy of Worship does not attempt to teach specific steps or proper ways to express our worship; rather it emphasizes the need to truly worship God. The method of worship, though important, differs according to individual tastes and interests.

Sammy Tippit writes poignantly from his heart and from his experience as an international evangelist and minister. Reading his words and sensing his excitement, the Christian is inspired all the more to worship the King of kings. There are rewards of worship, and Tippit's fresh presentation makes them real.

This book brings the reader to the foot of the throne and dramatically communicates the joy of being there. I heartily recommend it to Christians everywhere.

BILL BRIGHT
Founder and President
Campus Crusade for Christ International

Jesus was born of a virgin, suffered under Pontius Pilate, died on the cross, and rose from the grave to make worshipers out of rebels!

A. W. Tozer, *Whatever Happened to Worship*

O Come let us sing for joy to the Lord; Let us shout joyfully to the rock of our salvation; Let us come before His presence with thanksgiving; Let us shout joyfully to Him in Psalms. For the Lord is a great God, and a great King above all gods. . . . Come let us worship and bow down; Let us kneel before the Lord our Maker. For He is our God.

Psalm 95:1-3, 6-7*a*

1
A Call to Worship

During the summer of 1965 I knelt at the front of a large church in Baton Rouge, Louisiana. In those quiet moments, I bowed before the Creator and placed my trust and confidence in His Son, Jesus. My life has never been the same.

Many of my friends thought that I had simply had an emotional experience. They fully expected me to be back at the fraternity parties the next week on the university campus. I was well known for my partying spirit, heavy drinking of alcohol, and love of chasing women. One of my friends laughed at me after I received Jesus into my life. He said, "Tippit, I'll give you two weeks, and then you'll be back to the same old life. This religion stuff just doesn't work. It's all emotional. Forget about Jesus. We are going down to the beach this weekend. We will all get drunk and have a great time. Come with us."

I said to him, "I can't. I've met the Son of the living God. I've never met anyone like Him. I want to be at the church this weekend to worship Him. I don't understand everything. All I know is that He has changed me on the inside, and I love Him. He's so wonderful!"

My friend went to the beach and got drunk that weekend. The following Monday evening he called me on the telephone and asked, "Sammy, can you come over to my house? I need to talk with you." When I arrived at his home he told

9

me, "All I could think about this weekend was what you told me about Jesus. I need Jesus."

Together we knelt and prayed. He confessed his sinfulness and his need for the Savior. In those moments his life was radically changed. Both of us had been changed from rebels to worshipers of the King of glory. The next several months began the journey upon which I have traveled for the past twenty-four years.

It has been a journey upon which I have come to know intimately the One who is worthy of our worship. Every day I have come to appreciate, love, and revere Him more.

In those early days of my Christian faith I didn't know much about the Bible or about the nature of God. However, church services became thrilling to me. It was in them that I learned more about the Savior's love for me.

My friends and I began meeting together on a small hill overlooking a lake near the capitol building of our state. We read the Bible, memorized Scripture, and sought the face of God. Those were some of the most precious moments of my life. In them I began to discover who God is. And in those moments I learned to revere and worship Him.

Every holiday season gave me the opportunity to know and understand the Savior more fully. During my first Christmas season as a Christian I joined some friends for a prayer meeting in a small country church. It was such a thrill to comprehend for the first time the true meaning of Christmas. It became a season of worship rather than merely a time to buy, sell, give, and receive. How wonderful it was to be able to know the God who so loved us that He gave His Son.

Life took on an entirely new dimension. I had discovered why I was created: I was born to know, love, and worship the Lord God. I began to witness to my friends and colleagues—not as an obligation of the Christian life, but as an act of worship. I knew Him and simply wanted others to know Him.

One day in a public speaking class at the university, we were required to give an informative speech. We were to describe a person whom we had met, a book that we had read, or an event which we had attended. I spoke about the Person whom I had just met. I spoke of His attributes and characteristics, but I didn't tell who I was speaking about until the end of the speech. I concluded by saying, "He is the Creator of the universe. His name is Jesus." I was given a failing grade on the speech because the professor said that it was more an inspirational speech than an informative one. I left that class rejoicing that my professor had been inspired by the majesty of the God I had come to know.

It was in those formative days of my Christian life that I began to understand the joy, meaning, and principles of worship. I began to understand that the call of God upon our lives is a call to worship. The work of salvation in the heart of man turns rebellious, stubborn, self-willed persons into humble, obedient, worshiping saints.

The call to worship is universal and eternal. It is the call to all people in every tribe, nation, and generation. It is the highest call which can be made to an individual. It is the call of God to each of us, and as true worshipers, we must heed His call.

If we are to obey God's call to worship, we must understand some foundational truths about worship. First, we must understand the basis of true worship. True worship does not originate with the need of man but with the worthiness of God. Quite often it is said today that it really doesn't matter what one believes; it is only important that one believes. Such a philosophy indicates that the object of worship is not significant but that what really matters is only the act of worship.

This system of thought has been the tragedy of human history. Leaders have walked across the pages of history demanding allegiance and reverence. They have said to their generations, "Follow me." Some have been good leaders and others have been tyrants. But no human leader is worthy of worship and absolute loyalty. There is only one who stands out in history as worthy of our worship. His name is Jesus.

An old German Lutheran pastor once told me that during World War II he refused to "Hail Hitler!" He said that only Jesus is worthy of that kind of loyalty and reverence. He went to jail because he understood that real worship is rooted in the worthiness of the one to be worshiped. Many of the pastor's contemporaries thought he was foolish to refuse to worship a political leader. However, time and history have proved him correct. It is extremely important to know the character and essence of the one whom we worship.

I have traveled to many nations throughout the world, and in people of every culture I have discovered this same basic need to worship. It is present in the most obscure tribal people to the most sophisticated urbanites in the western world. There is something within man that says, "I want to know the unknown. There must be something bigger and greater than myself." People consequently find themselves worshiping gods of wood and stone, governments, gurus, or political and social leaders. The need to worship is one of the greatest needs of humanity.

A. W. Tozer said, "The yearning to know what cannot be known, to comprehend the Incomprehensible, to touch and taste the Unapproachable arises from the image of God in the nature of man. Deep calleth unto deep, and though polluted and landlocked by the mighty disaster theologians call the Fall, the soul senses its origin and longs to return to its Source."[1] However, there is a great problem common to the entire human race. The Bible says, "There is none righteous; not even one; there is none who understands, there is none who seeks for God. All have turned aside, together they have become useless; there is none who does good, there is not even one" (Romans 3:10-12).

Those are difficult words to swallow. But when we are really honest, we know that they are true. Sin has brought a curse upon humanity. It has distorted man's thought patterns, his emotions, and his ability to know God. There is a gap between our impure thoughts and the One who is absolute purity. It is impossible for us—we who live on emotional highs and lows—to comprehend Him. We are changeable, He changes not. We are inadequate, He is altogether adequate. We often make wrong decisions, but He alone is holy.

Thus, our entire moral nature has been affected by sin. Bishop J. C. Ryle, the outstanding nineteenth-century Christian writer and preacher said, "Sin is a disease which pervades and runs through every part of our moral constitution and every faculty of our minds. The understanding, the affections, the reasoning powers, the will, are all more or less infected."[2] Because of the fallen nature of man, worship has become distorted. It has become a means of covering up the dirt on the conscience of man rather than the expression of pure adoration and reverence for the Creator. Man has devised elaborate systems of worship and will go to great extremes to try to remove the stains of sin.

Once when I was preaching in India, I was traveling by auto to the city where I was scheduled to preach at evangelistic meetings. There were tens of thousands of people walking on the roads. I asked my Indian colleague where everyone was going. He said that they were all going to a Hindu temple about thirty miles away. I asked him why everyone was walking. My friend told me that they were trying to earn good "karma" (deeds) in hopes of a better future life. The more they sacrificed by walking, the more "karma" they earned. However, a person could walk completely around the earth, but it would not remove the stain of sin. Sin has left its mark on each of us. It is in our very nature, so every attempt at worship fails miserably.

In the western world there is much argument over the expression of true worship. Does a true worshiper lift his hands or remain quietly seated? Does he sing traditional hymns or modern choruses? I'm afraid that none of these things alone constitutes true worship. None of these activities can remove the stain of sin that is left on the soul of man.

Yet the stain of sin must be removed before we can comprehend the nature of true worship. God provided the way for our sins to be removed. He gave us His Son, Jesus, who lived a sinless, holy, perfect life. He died on a cruel cross, was buried, and arose from the grave. He ascended on high and is at the right hand of the heavenly Father. He is the historical Christ and the center of heavenly worship. It is His blood that can remove the stain of sin. It is through Jesus that we can experience true worship. It is by His grace that we are able to enter the presence of a holy God.

Thus, true worship does not originate with man. It originates with God. Worship is the result of the grace of God being applied to the heart of man; it flows from a heart that has been graced by God. The theme song for the true worshiper becomes, "Amazing grace, how sweet the sound that saved a wretch like me. I once was lost but now am found." I did not search so far and so wide that I found Him. I did not become so good that I could worship Him. He found me and graced me. Freely He forgave me, and freely I worship and love Him. It is not my style of worship nor my service for Him that makes me a true worshiper. It is His amazing grace.

After I saw that multitude of Hindus in India walking to their temple, I had the opportunity to speak to another large gathering of Hindus. I told them that I, too, had made a pilgrimage in life. I had searched for one who would be worthy of absolute allegiance and worship, and I had found no one. I told of the sense of guilt regarding my sin that had plagued me even though I desired to be a true worshiper. They listened intently as I said, "But one day my pilgrimage came to an end. The worthy One found me. His name is Jesus. He is God who came in human flesh. He is full of grace and truth. He is the pure, holy One who died for our sins. He arose from the grave to conquer death, and He extends His grace to you to cleanse you from every sin. By His grace, Jesus, the worthy One, can make you a true worshiper."

I was shocked when the Hindus began to applaud. It was good news to them. And it *is* good news to all people. True worship flows like a mighty river from the heart that has received God's grace. When we behold the Lamb of God who takes away the sins of the world, we become true worshipers.

This is the truth that over the centuries has stirred the Christian church to genuine worship. Count Ludwig von Zinzendorf, the great Moravian leader of the eighteenth century, was dramatically affected when he realized this beautiful truth. He saw a portrait of Christ with the inscription, "Christ dying on the cross." He looked at the picture and read, "I did this for thee, what wilt thou do for me?" The rest of his life Ludwig would confess, "I have but one passion, it is He and He alone."[3] When our hearts have been made clean by the love and grace of God, we too, will have but one passion: the love and adoration of the lovely Lord Jesus. Not long after I came to know God's love and forgiveness in Jesus, I was listening to a song which spoke of the nature of Jesus. It said that He, the Son of God, could have called ten legions of angels to take Him off the cross. But in His wonderful love, He died for us. That evening I went to a nearby lake and spent the rest of the evening in prayer. As I meditated on the cross, I could only weep. I thought of the infinite love that God has for us. Love and worship for Jesus began to pour forth from my heart as I realized that He is so wonderful.

I began to worship Him but not because I feared Him. Nor was it because I thought He would punish me if I didn't worship Him. I worshiped Him because He alone is the One worthy of my worship. And the worthy One loved me long before I ever considered worshiping Him. How good He is!

The Lamb of God is the center of worship in the book of Revelation, as the people of God gather around the throne of

God. There is one common denominator in all true worship: the Lamb of God who takes away the sins of the world.

So many times Christians are divided by forms of worship. We are divided by cultural, racial, generational, national, and denominational methods of worship. However, our unity as Christians will never be found in the exterior form of worship, but in the essence of our worship. Worship is rooted in who Jesus is. I am convinced that if we focus on Him, we will better love and appreciate one another. I travel quite often among different cultures, nationalities, ages, and racial groups. I have found people in all those groups whose lives have been changed by the marvelous grace of God. It is this grace that has made them true worshipers. I have learned to love and appreciate people of different backgrounds and forms of worship. It is the love that flows from the Lamb of God that brings us together and makes us one.

One day all of God's people—from every racial and ethnic origin and from every generation—will gather around God's throne. We will all sing the theme song, "Worthy is the Lamb." It will be interesting to learn of the work of grace in the hearts of so many saints throughout so many generations.

One of my hobbies is reading the biographies of the men and women of God of past generations. It is a reminder to me that God has not changed. He not only is the worthy One, but He always has been and always will be.

One man of God from the nineteenth century stands out as a trophy of God's grace. The Savior found Billy Bray. Because God's love poured over Billy's soul, he said, "I can't help praising the Lord."

Billy was a drunkard. He used to drink all night. He dreaded going to bed because he feared that he would wake up in hell. A friend once said of him, "He was the wildest, most daring and reckless of all the reckless, daring men."[4] After Jesus saved Billy from such a life, Billy had two constant companions: a Bible and a hymn book. He fell in love with the Savior. He could not help but worship Him.

Billy said concerning his salvation, "In an instant the Lord made me so happy that I cannot express what I felt. . . . I praised God with my whole heart for what He had done for a poor sinner like me."[5] Once Billy told a group of Christians, "I can't help praising the Lord! As I go along the street I lift up one foot, and it seems to say 'Glory!' and I lift up the other and it seems to say 'Amen'; and so they keep on like that all the time I am walking." To another group, he read the first line of a hymn by Charles Wesley, "O, for a thousand tongues to sing—" and then he would say, "Just think, that's 999 tongues more than I have got!"[6]

Billy Bray was one simple man who heeded the call of God upon his life. By the grace of God he was changed from a rebel to a worshiper. The call of God has not changed because the One worthy of our worship has not changed. If we are ever to discover the joy of worship that Billy Bray experienced, we must bow before Jesus, the Lamb of God. He will cleanse our sins and usher us into the presence of God. We will then humbly worship Him with our whole hearts saying, "Thou art worthy!"

NOTES

1. A. W. Tozer, *The Knowledge of the Holy* (New York: Harper & Row, 1961), p. 9.
2. J. C. Ryle, *Holiness* (1879; reprint, Grand Rapids, Mich.: Baker, 1979), p. 5.
3. Martyn Lloyd Jones, *The Cross* (Westchester, IL: Crossway, 1986), p. 61.
4. F. W. Bourne, *The Life of Billy Bray* (Monmouth, Gwent, U.K.: Bridge, 1987), p. 3.
5. Ibid., p. 6.
6. Ibid., pp. 24-25.

With our loss of the sense of majesty has come the further loss of religious awe and consciousness of the divine Presence. We have lost our spirit of worship and our ability to withdraw inwardly to meet God in adoring silence. . . . It is impossible to keep our moral practices sound and our inward attitudes right while our idea of God is erroneous or inadequate. If we would bring back spiritual power to our lives, we must begin to think of God more nearly as He is.

A. W. Tozer, *The Knowledge of God*

Then I said, "Woe is me, for I am ruined! Because I am a man of unclean lips, and I live among a people of unclean lips; for my eyes have seen the King, the Lord of hosts."

Isaiah 6:5

2
Spiritual Awakening and Worship

The great need in every generation is for a true knowledge of God. Without this knowledge the world loses its sense of meaning and the church falls into a state of apathy. Much of the church has fallen into that state today. There is a need for a great revival among God's people. Revival brings us as God's people back to our original purpose. It causes the Christian to worship God in simplicity and with devotion from the depths of his heart. The child of God is placed on the highway of holiness because he has tasted the holiness of God.

As the church prepares to enter the twenty-first century, it needs a fresh wind of revival. We must recapture that original purpose: to "love the Lord your God with all your heart, and with all your soul, and with all your mind" (Matt. 22:37). Many Christians in this generation are like the Ephesian Christians Jesus addressed in Revelation 2. The Ephesians had endured difficult circumstances and had remained orthodox in their faith. But Jesus told them that they needed to repent because they had left their first love. They needed the word of revival to rekindle in their hearts the flame of worship and adoration of the Lord Jesus.

Today it is not much different. There is evidence that the church in this generation needs a similarly great awakening. Five signposts point us to the need of that awakening.

SIGNPOST 1: HAVING AN IMPROPER VIEW OF CIRCUMSTANCES

The church of Ephesus had gone through great trials and difficult circumstances. Yet they had lost sight of the loveliness of the Lord Jesus in the midst of difficulties. Had they held Him near in those times of trouble, it could never have been said of them, "You have left your first love" (Rev. 2:4).

We, too, fail to hold the Lord near in our times of trouble. We need to heed the words of Thomas à Kempis, who said, "Shut thy door upon thee and call unto Jesus, thy love. When Jesus is nigh all goodness is nigh and nothing seemeth hard; but when He is not nigh all things are hard. If Jesus speaks one word, there is great comfort. To be without Jesus is a grievous hell, and to be with Jesus is a sweet paradise. If Jesus be with thee, there may be no enemy hurt thee."[1]

SIGNPOST 2: ALLOWING CIRCUMSTANCES TO OBSCURE GOD'S GLORY

God never promised that the Christian would ever be exempt from difficult circumstances. Hard times are to be expected. Trials will come to us as Christians. It is quite easy, however, for the Christian to lose his focus during the difficult times. It is easy for us to place all of our focus on circumstances and miss the beauty of Christ. We then begin to drift away from our first love. Worship of the worthy One becomes mundane, and we stand in the need of revival.

This principle was illustrated to me one day in Germany. I was staying in a small village in a mountainous area where it snowed often during the winter. I jogged regularly with a group of guys in the area. One day when we went out for our daily run, the ground was covered with about a foot of fresh snow. The first half hour of our run was complete drudgery. Fearful of tripping in the fresh snow, I trudged along, keeping my eyes on the ground. Every step became more difficult. I was at the point of exhaustion when I looked up.

I couldn't believe my eyes. I could see for miles. The houses, hills, trees, and roads were spotlessly white. Everything sparkled in the reflection of the sunlight. The view was magnificent, and I was awe-stricken. I decided to slow down, even walk, if necessary, in order to keep my eyes on the splendid scenery. A jog of absolute drudgery turned into one of immense delight. The difference was simply where I placed my focus.

Many Christians today have endured trials. Some of those believers have lost the joy of a Christian life because they have misplaced their focus. They have looked at their trials and difficulties for so long that the Christian life has become a drudgery. They need to slow down, stop, and behold the beauty of Jesus.

There are two things of which the Christian can be absolutely sure. First, there will be difficulties in the Christian life. Second, Jesus will be with him in those difficulties. The beauty and majesty of God can most clearly be seen in times of trouble. The child of God needs only to look up and see Christ's glory. The Christian does not need to ignore his trials as though they do not exist. He simply needs to recognize the sovereignty of God in the midst of his difficulties.

The deepest and purest moments of worship often come in the midst of trials and struggles. It is during those times that we come to appreciate the sufferings of Jesus. Therefore, we must learn to look unto Jesus during the difficult times of our lives.

Signpost 3: Seeking After Experiences

A third signpost pointing us toward our need of revival is our seeking after an aesthetic, spiritual experience rather than after a holy life. Nothing is wrong with having a deeply emotional experience of worship. But seeking after a praise-induced experience of worship so that one can have a superficial "feeling" of peace is not true worship.

This is not to say that a Christian will fail to experience peace when he worships. Joy and peace are natural by-products of worship. Joy is the fruit of coming into the presence of the Lord. Peace is a result of the Christian's correct relationship with God. We would be thrilled to receive an invitation to a private audience with Her Majesty Queen Elizabeth II. We would prepare carefully, dress properly, speak respectfully, and be grateful for the privilege of that meeting.

But there is an even greater thrill and excitement that comes with entering into the presence of the King of kings. One day the angels and all of the redeemed will cry out in beautiful harmony. "Hail to the King! Worthy is the Lamb!" Every knee will bow and every tongue confess that He is the Lord. That will be an awesome sight. But even now that same One, full of majesty and splendor, bids us daily to a private encounter with Him. We are called into the presence of the King, His Majesty the Lord Jesus Christ. We experience a sense of awe and wonder as we come before Him. He is the Creator of the universe and the Lord of life.

It is only "supernaturally" natural that the child of God should come into His presence with a sense of awe, wonder, and excitement. He will leave that encounter with a new twinkle in his eyes and a new spring in his steps.

Such an encounter will produce peace and joy in his life. Yet it is at this point that the child of God must be careful. Though many speak of the power of praise and the wonder of worship, I am convinced that there is no power in praise or wonder in worship. The power and wonder are in the majestic One. All power and honor and glory are His. The power of worship lies in Jesus Christ Himself, not in the method we use in coming into His presence. Many Christians worship God in only a superficial way because they do not understand this distinction. The distinction is not simply a matter of the words we use to describe worship, but has to do with what worship really is. If we are to have a correct understanding of worship, it is an extremely important distinction to keep in mind.

Much of the church has only touched the surface of true praise and worship because of an inadequate understanding of worship. We are not to worship "worship" or praise "praise." The purpose of worship is not to produce an ecstatic feeling or a peaceful state of mind. The purpose of worship is not to get something for ourselves. We worship because God alone is worthy of our worship.

This understanding liberates us in our worship experience and brings revival to our lives. We don't praise Him only because we feel like praising Him. We praise Him because we are entering into the presence of divine majesty. We worship Him because of who He is and not because of what we feel. That sets the Christian free in worship, because God does not change. Our feelings change. Our experiences change. But God remains the same. He always has been and always will be the great "I am." It doesn't matter if I wake up in a good mood or a bad mood. God is there. His nature is the same. He is the Rock that shall never be moved. We must conform our experience to His nature rather than attempt to conform His character to our experience.

A recent experience in Romania brought this truth home to me. I have preached in that country for several years, and the blessings of God have been bountiful each year. Some of my deepest friendships are in Romania. I have learned so much from Christian friends there. But on my last trip into that country, I experienced great difficulties.

The night before I left home for Romania I was in an automobile accident that totally demolished my car. No one was injured seriously in the accident, and I had received only minor cuts and bruises, but when I boarded the plane to fly to Europe I sat on the plane with a heavy heart. I had left my family without any transportation. I was lonely. I felt sorry for myself. I just didn't feel like worshiping God. However, the Holy Spirit kept reminding me of the words of that grand old hymn taken from the book of Lamentations: "Great is thy faithfulness. Great is thy faithfulness. Morning by morning new mercies I see. All I have needed, thy hand hath provided. Great is thy faithfulness, Lord, unto me."

The next day when I arrived in Budapest, Hungary, I was tired, but there was peace in my heart. Two Christian friends and I then boarded a train headed for the Romanian border. We separated on the train just in case any of us had problems at the border. That would prevent the others from also having difficulties.

The train arrived at the Romanian-Hungarian border at about 11:00 P.M. At midnight Romanian soldiers boarded the train and said, "Mr. Tippit, please take your luggage and come with us."

I asked the soldiers what was happening, but they refused to respond. They placed me under guard and kept me just outside the train station. A man from Poland was also being held under guard. He appeared to have been severely beaten.

My two friends were looking out the window as the train pulled away at 1:00 A.M. It was a sad moment for me. Tears welled up in my eyes. I lifted my hand and pointed my finger toward heaven. I knew that they had to depend upon God and not worry about me.

The next two hours were miserable. I had been traveling a day and a night without any sleep. I was tired, sore, and very lonely. I didn't know what was going to happen to me. I didn't know what my friends would face. I didn't know how my family was doing back in America. I only knew that it would be a long time before I saw my Romanian friends again. I began to question God in those moments. I questioned myself. Had God forsaken me? Or was I out of the will of God? Pity for myself welled up in me.

The sky was dark. The night was cold. By 3:00 A.M. my emotions were frazzled, and my body ached. To say the least, I didn't feel like worshiping God. But the Holy Spirit began to stir in my heart. That beautiful hymn began to rise within me and I began to sing, "Great is thy faithfulness. Great is thy faithfulness. Morning by morning new mercies I see. All I have needed thy hand hath provided. Great is thy faithfulness, Lord, unto me."

The guards looked at me as though I were crazy. I'm sure they couldn't understand why I was singing while I was their captive. It didn't make sense to me either. But in that moment I had a decision to make. I could become distraught and confused by my circumstances. I could fall prey to depression because of my emotions and feelings. Or I could look upon the loveliness of God. I could see Him as the Sovereign, caring King. The choice was mine.

I decided to place my focus on the faithfulness of God rather than on the fickleness of my feelings. I decided to give reverence to God rather than doubt my circumstances. One great hymn after another came to mind. I sang unto the Lord songs of praise and adoration for His attributes.

As I sang "Holy, Holy, Holy" and "How Great Thou Art," something remarkable transpired. It wasn't long before I forgot my problems. I held a little, private worship service. As I turned my attention away from my situation, I became secure in Christ. As I basked in the love and goodness of God, He allowed me to see the desperate plight of the guards holding me.

Then I began to sing to my guards in Romanian. For about an hour I preached the glorious gospel through singing. And the Holy Spirit gave me a tremendous insight. As long as I thought about my feelings, my circumstances, and my plight, I was defeated. Personal victory, peace, and joy were the fruit of the knowledge of God. I only had to worship Him. As I worshiped Him, I was able to witness to others. Then I walked in peace.

So many times we reverse that order. We seek after peace so that we can witness to others. Then we come to praise Him because of our experience. However, the wind of revival will bring us back to our first love. Our first love is not peace in our hearts. It is not our witness to the world. Our first love is God Himself. It is to God that we must return. As we return to our first love there will be a witness to the world and a walk of peace. Our experience will be the fruit of our worship. But only God will be the focus of our worship.

SIGNPOST 4: ORTHODOXY WITHOUT DEVOTION

There is a fourth signpost that reveals our need to return to our first love. It is the reverse of the previous one. It is orthodoxy without devotion. Many churches are filled with people who believe the right things about God but have lost their devotion to God. I once preached in a church in London where I was reminded of the need for whole-hearted devotion in our worship of God. At the conclusion of the service I was greeting people at the entrance of the church. A teenage girl leaving the church was wearing a coat that was covered with buttons. The buttons were filled with lots of funny sayings. But one of them simply said, "Boring!"

I thought to myself, *I have seen a lot of Christians leave churches without any buttons, but they have had "boring" written across their hearts and faces.* Great damage has been done to the name of Christ by half-hearted, lukewarm Christians who appear to be worshiping. It is this type of worship that will cause the church to lose the battle for the souls of future generations. It is absolutely outrageous that we teach our children that the place where we worship Jesus Christ is the place where we catch an hour's nap during the worship time.

The church of Laodicea is described as one that was neither hot nor cold. It was lukewarm. God said to them, "I will spit you out of My mouth" (Rev. 3:16). Half-hearted, lukewarm worship breaks the heart of God because it is not true worship. Many claim to believe that Jesus is the "Wonderful Counselor, Mighty God, Eternal Father, Prince of Peace" spoken of by the prophet Isaiah (9:6) yet only irreverently and half-heartedly tip their hats to Him one hour of the week. Theirs is perhaps the worst form of hypocrisy in which a Christian can involve himself.

A wind of revival must blow across the children of God to reawaken us to the glory of the Lord Jesus. If we are to be true worshipers, we must embrace with our whole hearts the fact that our only hope is Jesus. We will then be renewed in our faith and walk with God. The great men of God in past years have been men who were both orthodox and deeply devoted to the Lord Jesus. One of them was George Whitefield, who was mightily used in the first Great Awakening in America. Bishop J. C. Ryle said of him, "He was a man of burning love to our Lord Jesus Christ."[2]

SIGNPOST 5: A LACK OF HOLINESS

The final signpost that points a Christian toward his need for revival is a lack of holiness in the life. The men and women of the Bible who became genuine worshipers of God were those who encountered the holiness of God. When Moses met God on the mountain he was told, "Do not come near here; remove the sandals from your feet, for the place on which you are standing is holy ground" (Exodus 3:5). Isaiah had a vision of God in which the angels cried out, "Holy, Holy, Holy is the Lord of hosts, the whole earth is full of His glory" (Is. 6:3). David asked the question, "Who may ascend into the hill of the Lord? And who may stand in His holy place?" and he answered it, as well: "He who has clean hands and a pure heart" (Psalms 24:3-4).

When we come into the presence of God, we are coming into the presence of perfect purity. God is holy. When we come before Him, we must come with a commitment in our hearts to holiness of life. Worship of God comes from a heart that is in the process of becoming like Christ.

Bishop Ryle defined holiness when he wrote, "True holiness, we surely ought to remember, does not consist merely of inward sensations and impressions. It is much more than tears, and sighs, and bodily excitement, and a quickened pulse, and a passionate feeling of attachment to our own favorite preachers and our own religious party, and a readiness to quarrel with every one who does not agree with us. It is something of the image of Christ, which can be seen and observed by others in our private life, and habits, and character, and doings."[3]

Thus, our worship must be wrapped in a life that is becoming like Christ. A growing Christian will be a worshiping Christian, and a worshiping Christian will be a growing Christian. The heart is what counts in worship. The heart that has beheld Jesus and is surrendered to Him is the heart that is able to worship.

There is much talk of renewal of worship in this generation. If we are truly to obtain that renewal, we must fix our hearts on the Lord Jesus. He alone must be the object of our worship. We desperately need the wind of revival to blow across our hearts, restoring us to our original purpose of loving Him and becoming like Him.

Notes

1. As quoted in Warren Wiersbe, *Listening to the Giants* (Grand Rapids, Mich: Baker, 1980), p. 101.

2. J. C. Ryle, *Christian Leaders of the 18th Century* (Edinburgh: Banner of Truth, 1885), p. 57.

3. J. C. Ryle, *Holiness* (1879; reprint, Grand Rapids, Mich.: Baker, 1979), p. xv.

Jesus is not one of the group of the world's great. Talk about Alexander the Great and Charles the Great and Napolean the Great if you will . . . Jesus is apart. He is not the Great; He is the Only. He is simply Jesus. Nothing could add to that.

Carnegie Simpson,
in *Basic Christianity*

And I began to weep greatly, because no one was found worthy to open the book, or to look into it; and one of the elders said to me, "Stop weeping; behold, the Lion that is from the tribe of Judah, the Root of David, has overcome so as to open the book and its seven seals.

And they sang a new song saying, "Worthy art Thou to take the book, and to break its seals; for Thou wast slain, and didst purchase for God with Thy blood men from every tribe and tongue and people and nation."

Revelation 5:4-5, 9

3
Worthy of Worship

Jesus is unique in human history. He is not merely one of the gods. He is God. He is not just a good man. He is the only man who is perfect in His goodness. He is not only a great leader. He is the only leader worthy of absolute devotion and allegiance. He is not only royalty, but He is the King of kings and the Lord of lords. Jesus is holy, righteous, and eternal. John called Him the Son of God, and Luke called Him the Son of Man. He is the God-man. He is in a class all His own.

The great search of the human heart is the search to discover the One who is worthy of our worship. Margaret Cleator, in *The God Who Answers by Fire,* tells the story of a young man in India, Arjun, who made such a pilgrimage.[1] He began his journey as the consequence of a great tragedy in his family. He had been away from home, studying in the university. When he graduated, he returned to his home—and there, as he walked into the house, he heard his mother screaming, "She's dead! She's dead!" Arjun's sister, Tara, had become ill and died. Her death left Arjun in a state of shock and despair. He decided that he must find answers to life's most basic questions.

Arjun set out on a journey to the great temples of India. He wanted to know God and find some reasons for his sister's life and death. For one entire year, he visited temple after temple. At the first temple he visited, he spoke with a yogi and said, "Swamiji, I have a question to ask."

The yogi only replied, "You have no offering?"

Arjun apologetically said, "I have no money."

With a stare into space the yogi said, "You come into the presence of God with empty hands."

It was then that Arjun realized that he would need money to give to the religious leaders when he asked them for the answers to his questions. He responded quietly, "I wanted to ask you if you have found God." The yogi gave no answer and Arjun left.

The months that followed were depressing for Arjun. No one was able or willing to tell him how to find God. He even met a priest who had studied at Oxford in Great Britain. The priest told him that he could only find God as he was "absorbed into his essence as a drop of water is absorbed into the ocean." He told Arjun to memorize the thousand names, titles, and epithets of Vishnu, a Hindu deity, and to stand in the Ganges River at midnight with water up to his neck, repeating those names. Then he would become one with God.

Arjun obeyed the priest only to realize that the priest had given him a command to commit suicide. The river's current was so swift that Arjun almost drowned while screaming the names and titles of Vishnu. He was saved by a temple prostitute the very moment before the current swept him away. The prostitute threw a rope to him and brought him safely to the shore.

Arjun regained consciousness on the shore and continued his desperate search for God. However, no religious leader could tell him how to find God. After a year of searching, he finally gave up. He headed back to his home, very despondent.

While Arjun was walking homeward, a common man in a bullock-driven cart asked him if he would like a ride. The man asked Arjun why he looked so downcast. Arjun told him of his search for God and how he had not found Him. This common man told Arjun that he had found God five years earlier. He told him that the only way really to know

God was through the God-man, Jesus. He spoke of the purity of Jesus and of His love for all men. Arjun learned that Jesus was not like the religious leaders he had met on his pilgrimage. He learned that Jesus is full of grace rather than greed. And Jesus offered him life rather than death. But most of all he learned that God is holy. Arjun already knew that he was sinful. Now he learned that Jesus had died on the cross as the penalty for his sins.

Arjun spent much time with his new friend. He read the Bible and observed his friend's quality of life. Then one day Arjun bowed before Jesus as the worthy One and received Him into his life as Lord and Savior. At last he cried out, "I've found Him! Oh, I've found Him! He's made me clean. I've got peace at last!"

Arjun had searched throughout his country to find God, but he could not find Him. However, when Arjun came to the end of his own means, God found Arjun.

I believe Arjun's search expresses the desire in the heart of every person who has ever lived. At some point in every one of our lives we have wanted deeply to know if there is a God and how we can have a relationship with Him. I have met young people in Eastern Europe who have been taught all their lives that there is no God. Yet deep within themselves they still have a yearning to know God. Others have sought openly for God in the western world only to become disillusioned with greedy religious manipulators. These searchers point to the inconsistency of some Christian ministers and, like Arjun, give up their search.

However, there is One who is unique in human history. He alone is worthy of worship. He is not like any of the gods of this world. Nor is He like those who use His name for their own selfish ambitions. He is Jesus, God manifested in human flesh. The book of Hebrews describes Jesus as "the radiance of His glory and the exact representation of His nature" (Heb.1:3). To know, love, and worship Jesus is to know, love, and worship God.

Such a bold claim can be made on the basis of the clear distinction between Jesus and all other men. Jesus is different from all other men in His character, His claims, and the confirmations that attended His life.

THE CHARACTER OF CHRIST

Jesus is not only the purest man ever to live—He *is* purity. He is not just another holy man in human history—He *is* holiness. Jesus cannot be characterized as some sort of superstar. His life can only be described as supernatural.

There are four historical accounts of the life of Jesus in the Bible. In each account we discover one ray of the radiance of God's glory as revealed in the character of Christ. Matthew, a Jewish tax collector, wrote of the majesty of Jesus. He recognized royalty in the life and character of Christ. He understood that Jesus was worthy of worship because of His royal nature.

Matthew presents Jesus as the promised Messiah, the "anointed One." Jesus was the One for whom the Jews had been waiting for hundreds of years. Jesus was not King of the Jews because the Jewish people needed a revolutionary leader to deliver them from their hardships under Roman rulership. He was King of the Jews because He was the promised One. He was the fulfillment of one thousand years of prophecy about the Messiah.

Jesus was of royal lineage. Matthew refers to Jesus nine times as the "son of David." He traces the historical roots of Jesus back to King David. He writes of the miraculous birth of Jesus as well as of the obscure place of His birth, both of which were fulfillments of prophecies concerning the Messiah. Jesus was the majestic One.

There has never been a king like King Jesus. Royalty is to be served. Yet this King did not come to be served, but He came to serve. He did not come with great ego needs, but He came to lay His life down for all humanity. He is the King who served the people.

Mark, who spent much time with the apostles Peter and Paul, wrote of the servanthood of Jesus. He omits the birth and early life of Jesus in his gospel account. He opens his account by introducing Jesus at His baptism. He allows the reader to see immediately the beauty of King Jesus as the Servant-Redeemer. Mark quotes Jesus as saying, "For even the Son of Man did not come to be served, but to serve, and to give His life a ransom for many" (Mark 10:45).

Many kings have walked across the pages of human history, but never one like King Jesus. He is altogether unique in His character. He is full of majesty, yet truly humble. He has all authority in heaven and on earth. Yet He is the servant of men. He is the King of kings. Yet He took off His royal robes to give His life as a sacrifice for the sin of rebellious mankind.

Luke presents another aspect of the nature of God and the beauty of His glory that are found in Jesus. Luke speaks often of Jesus as the Son of Man—but Jesus is not like any other man who has ever lived. All other men must confess, "I have sinned." But Jesus was the perfect Man. Only a perfect human could save a sinful humanity. Jesus said, "The Son of Man has come to seek and save that which was lost" (Luke 19:10). John Stott, a British scholar and gospel minister, said of Jesus, "All other men were sick with the disease of sin; He was the doctor who had come to heal them. All other men were plunged in the darkness of sin and ignorance; He was the light of the world."[2]

Jesus was perfect in His compassion. No one else has ever loved people like He loved them. He loved the lonely, the hurting, and the afflicted. He loved the poor as well as the powerful. He loved His friends, who forsook Him, and His enemies, who crucified Him. In His darkest moment, while He hung on the cross, He prayed, "Father, forgive them; for they do not know what they are doing" (Luke 23:34). No man ever loved like the Man, Christ Jesus. And it was not just that He loved people with a great love—He *was* love. Jesus was the perfect Man.

However, Jesus was more than perfect in His humanity. He was, is, and always will be divine. He is God. Thus, though Luke focuses on the beauty of Jesus as that of the Perfect Man, John describes the glory of Jesus as that of the God-Man. Luke speaks of Jesus as the Son of Man; John writes of Jesus as the Son of God.

The glory of God is revealed in Jesus, the eternal One. John quotes Jesus as saying, "Truly, truly, I say to you, before Abraham was born, I am" (John 8:58). Abraham lived hundreds of years before the time of Christ. Yet Jesus claimed His existence before the time of Abraham. John testifies that Jesus was "in the beginning."

Not only does John paint a portrait of Christ as being the eternal One, he also portrays Jesus as the almighty One. He describes Jesus' power over both life and death. Jesus walked up to the tomb of a friend who had recently died, and He made a phenomenal statement: "I am the resurrection and the life; he who believes in Me shall live even if he dies" (John 11:25). Then He called the dead man, Lazarus, to come back to life. And Lazarus had life breathed into his body, and he was resurrected.

There is no one who has ever lived who is like Jesus. He is full of majesty and owns the title "King of kings." But He shed His royal garments in order that He might wear the garments of a servant. Yet He is much more than the King who became a servant. He is the eternal, almighty God who took upon Himself human flesh. He was the perfect Man. He is unique among all persons who have ever walked this planet, for He is the God-Man and the Servant-King. When one looks into the historical accounts of the life, character, and essence of Jesus, he must fall on his face and cry out, "You alone are worthy of worship."

Christianity is different from other religions because it is not just a system of beliefs or a philosophical view of life. One could take Mohammed out of Islam and it would remain a great religion. The same is true with Buddha and many of the other great religions of the world. However, it is not true with Christianity. Christianity is Christ. Jesus is not just a good moral teacher or one of the great prophets of the ages; He is God in the flesh. The essence of Christian worship is not in its form or its style. Nor is Christianity a system of philosophical teachings about good works. The essence of Christian worship is in the person of Jesus Christ. Worship flows from a genuine understanding of the character of Jesus. When one truly comprehends that, worship will flow from us to the Father because of the Son.

THE CLAIMS OF CHRIST

Jesus is different from all others in human history not only because of His nature but also because of His claims. The character of Christ provides a foundation for His claims. If He was not a man of absolute moral purity, His claims would be completely absurd. But to the contrary, because of His moral purity and integrity, we must take His claims seriously. We have no other choice.

C. S. Lewis, the great Christian philosopher and author, had this to say of Jesus' claims: "A man who was merely a man and said the sort of things Jesus said would not be a great moral teacher. He would either be a lunatic on the level with the man who says he is a poached egg—or else he would be the Devil of Hell. You must make your choice. Either this man was, and is, the Son of God; or else a madman or something worse. You can shut Him up for a fool, you can spit at Him and kill Him as a demon; or you can fall at His feet and call Him Lord and God. But let us not come with any patronising nonsense about His being a great human teacher. He has not left that open to us. He did not intend to."[3]

What were the claims of Christ? Who did Jesus say He was? Those may be difficult questions for twentieth-century readers to answer. However, they were not difficult for those closest to Him—those who ate with Him, walked with Him, and listened to His teachings. He claimed to be deity. There was no doubt in the disciples' minds about that. Those closest to Him were willing to love and obey Him, were willing even to die to proclaim that He was and is God in human flesh.

Not only were His closest associates sure that He claimed to be God, but His most bitter enemies were positive that those were His claims as well. He was asked by Caiaphas, the Jewish high priest, "Are you the Christ, the Son of the Blessed One?" And Jesus said, "I am; and you shall see the Son of Man sitting at the right hand of power, and coming with the clouds of heaven" (Mark 14:61-62). There was no doubt in the high priest's mind as to what Jesus had just said. He claimed to be the Messiah. Caiaphas was so outraged that he tore his clothes and said, "What further need do we have of witnesses? You have heard the blasphemy; how does it seem to you?" (Mark 14:63-64). Everyone agreed, so He was condemned to death. The claim of Christ was clear to friends and foes alike: He claimed to be God.

Either Jesus was a man who made Himself out to be God, or He truly was God who became man. Those are the only two choices concerning Christ that we have available to us. Jesus was pure in His moral character, yet He claimed to be God. Therefore, we must deny His moral purity or we must bow before Him in worship and adoration.

The Confirmation of Christ

There was a man in the New Testament who had one great purpose in life: to prepare the way for the coming Messiah. He preached repentance and baptized multitudes in the Jordan River. Then he was cast into prison. While there, he sent two of his disciples to inquire about Jesus. They asked Jesus directly, " 'Are you the Expected One, or shall we look for someone else?' And Jesus answered and said to them, 'Go and report to John what you hear and see: the blind receive sight and the lame walk, the lepers are cleansed and the deaf hear, and the dead are raised up, and the poor have the gospel preached to them' " (Matthew 11:3-5).

The response of Jesus was quite clear. He was not only absolute moral purity. He not only claimed to be God. His very works confirmed His character and claims. Today, as then, Jesus' works defy us to write Him off as some sort of lunatic or even as one of the great moral leaders of the world, for no one has ever done what Jesus did. With one word from His lips the winds ceased, the seas were stilled, the lame walked, the blind saw, and the dead came back to life. That is not the work of a crazy man. Nor was it the work of merely a great man. Only one conclusion can possibly be drawn. His work was—and is—the work of the God-Man.

However, the works of Christ are not the greatest confirmation that He is worthy of our worship. He kept telling His disciples that He had to go to Jerusalem and die. He said that He would rise from the dead on the third day. And it happened exactly as He said it would. Herein lies the greatest of the confirming works of Jesus.

Many great leaders have sincerely loved and served their people. But Jesus was, and is, different from all other leaders in history. First, He did not die just for friends and family. He died for friends, family, and *foes*. He loved with a supernatural love.

I once had a friend in college for whom I thought there was no hope. One day he would act like a Christian and the next day he would blaspheme God. He once knelt and challenged God. "God," he cried out, "if there be a God, then strike me dead." Immediately he came to my dormitory room to convince me that there was no God. I honestly felt there was no hope for that guy. One day several years later I ran into my friend. He told me, "I don't know how Jesus could have loved and died for someone like me. But I'm so thankful He did. I've given my heart to Him, and I now love and follow Him."

We were all rebels when Jesus loved us. Many leaders have given their lives for their friends. But only Jesus had the capacity to love all men. He is the lover of our souls when there is nothing lovely in our souls. When we embrace the old rugged cross by faith, our hearts are turned from rebellion to worship.

Jesus differs from all other leaders in history in another way: He was resurrected from the dead. Other great leaders have lived and died for their people, but Jesus conquered death itself and now offers life to whomever believes in Him. I recall standing one wintry evening in Red Square in Moscow in front of the tomb of Lenin. Thousands of people gather there daily to view the body of Lenin, which has been preserved by the Soviet Union. As I stood in front of that tomb I recalled the words of Jesus when He said, "I am the resurrection and the life." I had a private worship service right there in Red Square. I knew that Jesus was not just another name among the great names of history. His is the name above all names. He stands out in human history as Immanuel, God with us. And He is certainly with us. He has conquered man's worst enemies: death, hell, and the devil. He alone is worthy of our worship.

When Thomas, the doubting disciple of Jesus, understood that Jesus was truly risen from the dead, he cried out, "My Lord and my God." When Saul, the hater of Christians, beheld the resurrected Christ, he became Paul, the bond servant of Jesus. When we recognize Jesus as the Servant-King and the God-Man, we will likewise bow in humble submission and reverence to Him as our Lord and our God.

NOTES

1. Margaret Cleator, in *The God Who Answers by Fire* (Kent, England: STL Books, 1966), pp. 10, 32-33, 70.

2. John Stott, *Basic Christianity* (Downers Grove, Ill.: InterVarsity, 1980), p. 37.

3. C. S. Lewis, *Mere Christianity* (New York: MacMillan, 1952), p. 56.

Look at the things of this world—wives, children, possessions, estates, power, friends, and honor; how amiable are they! How desirable to the thoughts of the most of men! But he who has obtained a view of the glory of Christ will, in the midst of them all, say, "Whom have I in heaven but thee? And there is none upon the earth that I desire beside thee" (Ps. 73:25 KJV*).

John Owen,
Glory of Christ

No one can serve two masters; for either he will hate the one and love the other, or he will hold to one and despise the other. You cannot serve God and mammon.

Matthew 6:24

*King James Version

4
False Worship

Jesus is the incomparable Christ. True worship will always be wholehearted worship built upon the single foundation of the glory of Christ. Everyone and everything else are too superficial and finite to command our absolute loyalty. It is impossible to worship Jesus and also bow to the gods of our culture.

What would a wife think of a husband with dual loyalties? She would not be very pleased if he came home from work one day and said, "Sweetheart, I love you. I really do. I love you more than any other person in this world. As a matter of fact, I love you so much that I am going to live with you more than I live with the two beautiful women I met at the office. I will live with you and be loyal only to you five days out of every week. Then I will love and be loyal to the other two women the two remaining days of the week. You see, I love you more than both of them put together."

I don't think that his comments would be very comforting to his wife. She might say, "Make up your mind. It is me or them. You can't have it both ways."

That is exactly what Jesus meant when He said, "No one can serve two masters" (Matt. 6:24). There are many in the church today who say, "I love and worship Jesus." They give intellectual assent to the beauty and glory of Jesus. However, they hold back a part of their hearts for the gods of their culture. They claim to have an altar of worship built to Jesus in their hearts, but close inspection reveals that in their hearts are several other altars.

Dual loyalties and multiple objects of worship have been great problems for God's people throughout the centuries. In the Old Testament the nation of Israel continually struggled to maintain its single-minded devotion and loyalty to Jehovah. During the mid-700s B.C. they enjoyed a temporary time of prosperity. But the hearts of the people were riddled with sin and idolatry. Israel was called out and set apart as God's own people. But they committed spiritual adultery. They ran after other gods.

During that time God raised up a prophet to call the people back to wholehearted worship of Himself. Hosea, whose name means "salvation," was given that task. His assignment was a difficult one. God required of him that he marry a prostitute and have children by her. That woman, Gomer, prostituted herself with other men, just as the children of Israel prostituted themselves with the worship of other gods. God intended Hosea's relationship with Gomer to be an illustration of the tragedy of God's people whose hearts were divided in their worship.

Their divided devotion brought three tragic consequences upon them. Christians who leave room in their hearts for the gods of this culture will find the same tragic results in their own lives. In Hosea 4:1-7 the Scriptures outline the consequences of false worship among God's people.

Consequences of False Worship

The first consequence of false worship is the loss of the respect of others. God spoke through the prophet Hosea, saying, "The more they multiplied, the more they sinned against Me; I will change their glory into shame" (Hosea 4:7). The Israelites had experienced prosperity, but they had forgotten who had prospered them. They had grown numerically but not spiritually: they did not glorify and worship God in the midst of that numerical growth. They only sinned more.

Among evangelicals today the philosophy seems to be "big is better." We seem to think that what pleases God is simply to have bigger churches and a greater number of people in our congregations. It *is* wonderful to have an evangelistic, growing church. It *is* great to have financial blessings in our churches. It *is* glorious to have ten thousand people who love God with their whole hearts in church on Sunday. But having a larger congregation or a bigger budget does not constitute true worship. Rather, it is a terrible shame to have ten thousand people who love Jesus two days a week and two other gods the other five days. At any moment the glory of a church, a nation, or an individual can become a sham.

The young person who worships Jesus but also bows to the god of "popularity" may lose the respect of other students. The businessman who praises God on Sunday but compromises his ethics on Monday will probably not command the respect of his colleagues. The minister who proclaims the kingdom of God but builds his own empire will ultimately lose the respect of his congregation. We cannot bow to the gods of "silver," "sex," and "self-glory" and worship Jesus at the same time.

Though the cradle of Christianity was the Middle East, after a point the focus of Christian endeavor shifted to the West. It is in the West that the church grew, and it is from the West that missionaries have gone to assignments throughout the world. But today, the church in the West has lost much of the respect it once had. The nations of the world can see that western Christians have tried to embrace Christianity and secularism at the same time. They have bowed to the gods of western society at the same time they have tried to serve Christ. We in the west have lost our saltiness, and our light has been dimmed. We have lost the respect of those whom we most desire to reach with the message of Christ.

The *Wall Street Journal* carried a series of articles by James Sterba about the rise of Islam throughout the world. Sterba described the process many young people in Indonesia have followed in their turning to Islam. The first step is one of disillusionment. "Amid drugs, pollution, pornography, greed and lawlessness, young Indonesians—especially those who have studied abroad—find much in Western society that is sick and disturbing. Returning from the culture shock of education in the U.S. and Europe, students feel like misfits."[1] The second step is one of resolution. "Frustrated" by what they have seen of western religion, the young Indonesians "have turned to Islam," Sterba says, quoting another journalist who has studied the phenomenon.[2]

Many Christians may respond smugly to such an article by saying, "Those young Indonesians rejected our society, not the churches in our society." It would be nice if that were totally true. It would be wonderful if the Christian church in western Europe and North America were distinctively different from their respective societies. However, I spoke recently at an international conference where a young man from Pakistan pleaded for the Christians at the conference to pray for the Christians in his country. They were being ridiculed by the media because of the scandalous sins of Christian leaders in America. Christians in our churches should weep and repent over the altars that we have built to false gods. As we repent, our reputation will be restored.

The second consequence of false worship is the loss of one's children. The children of Israel lost much more than the respect of others when they worshiped other gods in their society. They lost their children. Hosea brought a word from God when he said, "Since you have forgotten the law of your God, I will also forget your children" (Hosea 4:6). A heart divided in its loyalties will produce a home divided in its worship.

Parents have a tremendous responsibility to love God with their whole hearts. One of the most destructive forces in a Christian home is inconsistency in the lives of parents.

When I first began to preach the gospel of Christ, I was working with young people on the streets. Many of them were runaways, dropouts, and drug users. My ministry began in the late sixties among the young people in the counter-culture called hippies. This was the "baby boomer" generation that had rejected the traditional values of their parents.

As I preached the glorious gospel of Christ among my contemporaries, I discovered something very frightening. Many of these young people came from solid, evangelical churches and families. I met the children of deacons, pastors, and elders. I asked many of them why they had left their homes and rejected the God of their fathers. In about 75 percent of the cases these young people spoke of the inconsistencies in their parents' lives. Their parents were faithful on Sundays to sing the grand hymns of praise and adoration of the Savior. Yet it was obvious that they had built altars to other gods, also. Instead of the pursuit of God, their time and energies were spent in the pursuit of power, prestige, and wealth. Consequently, those parents lost their children.

At the time that my wife and I discovered that she was pregnant with each of our children, we held a prayer meeting. We dedicated each of the children to the Lord. We knew that the call of God upon our lives was to worship and honor Him. Therefore, we wanted to honor Him with our children. In dedicating our children to the Lord, we were in reality dedicating ourselves to a life of wholehearted worship of God.

Actually, the prayer of dedication was the easy part of rearing our children. The difficult part has been to live before them in such a manner that they will want to follow the God that we love and worship. It is so easy to compromise and embrace the gods of our culture. There is much pressure from society to conform, and there is the subtle appeal of false worship. Our children face tremendous pressure to prostitute themselves to the glitzy gods of our society. But if we want to rear godly children and not lose them to the world, we must not bow to the gods of this generation. They must see and experience the security that dwells in a home where only the God of Abraham, Isaac, and Jacob is worshiped.

The third consequence of divided worship is the loss of power in ministry. Hosea said, "My people are destroyed for lack of knowledge. Because you have rejected knowledge, I will also reject you from being My priest" (Hosea 4:6). Earlier he had explained what knowledge it was that they had rejected: "There is no faithfulness or kindness or knowledge of God in the land" (Hosea 4:1).

The Israelites no longer had the power to minister as priests because they had rejected the knowledge of God. This is perhaps the most tragic of all the consequences of a divided heart. The Christian who bows to the gods of the age loses his power to minister because he loses his knowledge of God. The great need of every generation is for men and women who really know God. I am convinced that our churches do not need to be filled with more people, but rather the people who are already in our churches need to be filled with the knowledge of God. When we have an intimate knowledge of God, our churches will not have room to contain the people who will be seeking the God we know.

We have thought for too long that the power to reach the world for Christ is in a hip, Hollywood-style evangelism. We must learn that the world is not looking for a slick, sensational form of Christianity. The world basically needs to see reality in our Christianity. That reality comes from people who have a genuine knowledge of God. And it is impossible really to get to know God intimately while we worship the gods of the age.

This generation needs men and women of character, and the root of godly character is a true knowledge of God. As we get to know Him, we will come to love Him. As we love Him, we will obey Him. Obedience is simply the knowledge of God applied to daily living. The fruit of that knowledge is power in ministry. Ministry is an outgrowth of character. If we are on the growing edge of becoming like Christ, we will have power in ministry. If we are not becoming like Christ, we will be powerless to help others to know Christ. Therefore, we must be very careful never to lose that intimate knowledge of God—but we will not know that intimacy with God as long as we cling to the gods of our culture.

THE GODS OF THE AGE

Every generation and culture builds its own idols, and this generation is no different. There are four gods that are obvious in these days. It is interesting to note that in many of the scandals of the Christian church in recent years, one or more of these "gods" has been associated with the scandals.

The first is the "god of pleasure." Webster defines hedonism as "the doctrine that pleasure is the principal good and should be the aim of action." Much of the modern world has become hedonistic in its thinking, and it has built altars everywhere to the god of pleasure.

The church likewise has become hedonistic in her approach to worship. As I have traveled internationally, my heart has broken over the plight of many Christians. Too many "born again" Christians think that they have worshiped God if they leave their churches Sunday morning with a few pleasurable feelings. Their objective in worship is self-gratification rather than God-glorification. Pleasure rather than purity has become the test of worship for them.

But Jesus said, "Blessed are the pure in heart, for they shall see God" (Matt. 5:8). I once witnessed to two homosexuals at the conclusion of a worship service. They told me that they would not come back to the church because they felt uncomfortable in the services. They attended another church where their homosexual practices were not an issue. They could sing praises, worship, and feel good during those services without altering their lifestyles.

In essence, those two young women were not worshiping the God of the Bible. They were worshiping the god of pleasure: if it feels good, do it. Much worship today is in tandem with that philosophy. It is little more than an attempt to make people feel good. Yet we will not always feel comfortable when we come into the presence of a holy God. His presence and glory will expose our sin. Repentance is not easy. It is difficult. Often God must bring us to the place where we are deeply sorrowful over our sins.

The second false god we have come to worship is the "god of possessions." Somehow we have come to think that the "chief end of man is to glorify God" *and* to accumulate as many things as possible. We have defined success in this generation in terms of budgets, buildings, and big business. We have come to think that the sum total of life lies in our possessions, so we have fallen at the altars of materialism.

One does not have to be wealthy to worship the "god of possessions." I have met many middle and low income people, as well as wealthy persons, who have bowed to this god. It is not money that is the root of all evil. It is the *love* of money (1 Tim. 6:10). We live in a material world, but we are to use our material possessions for the glory of God and the advancement of His kingdom.

The god of possessions can be subtle in luring our hearts. Many Christians have begun their journey in Christ with wholehearted devotion to God. Then, somewhere along the way, they have lost their perspective and have begun to bow before this false god.

How can a Christian detect the lure of the god of possessions? He can detect it when he realizes that he is determining his worth and value by his possessions. That is the point at which he has begun to worship at the altar of this false god. He can detect the subtle trap also when he realizes that he has begun to ascribe importance to others on the basis of their posessions. When he has begun to do that, he will have divided his heart between the cultural god and the true God.

James 2:2-4 gives a strong warning in this matter: "For if a man comes into your assembly with a gold ring and dressed in fine clothes, and there also comes in a poor man in dirty clothes, and you pay special attention to the one who is wearing the fine clothes, and say, 'You sit here in a good place,' and you say to the poor man, 'You stand over there, or sit down by my footstool,' have you not made distinctions among yourselves, and become judges with evil motives?"

Many in this generation have fallen into the trap of ascribing importance only to people with wealth. We have wrongly defined success. The successful pastor or Christian worker is not necessarily the one with the biggest church facility, the biggest home, or the biggest automobile. The successful Christian worker is the one who has been faithful in his service to God and has given wholehearted worship to Him. It is to such a worker that God will one day say, "Well done, thou good and faithful servant." Our worth and value must be found in God alone. We must not worship at the altar of the god of possessions. Our worth can only be found in the One who is worthy of our worship.

The third false god that must be removed from our lives is the "god of prestige." We must make a choice. It is either "not I, but Christ who lives in me," or it is "self" and not Christ who reigns in my life. We cannot build monuments and shrines to ourselves while we claim to worship Jesus. A true worshiper is the one who seeks the kingdom of God, not the one who is building his own empire. The hunger of the true worshiper will be for the kingdom of God and His righteousness. He will not have room in his heart for a monument to man or for an attitude of self-righteousness.

Many mighty ministers in recent years have fallen. On several occasions Proverbs describes the root cause of the fall of a man. It says, "A man's pride will bring him low, but a humble spirit will obtain honor" (Prov. 29:23). Pride is a dangerous thing. It has a way of creeping into the hearts of even the most spiritual of men.

When we experience the blessings of God, we face our greatest temptation. The most dangerous times of our Christian lives come after the great victories that we have experienced. When we have fought and won the battles, we are tempted to build an altar to the "god of prestige." When we receive praise, we stand in the great moment of decision. In that moment we must humbly receive the praise accorded us and then lay it at the feet of Jesus. We must never believe that we are as great as everyone says we are.

We must consciously acknowledge that we are what we are only by the grace of God. Solomon wisely wrote, "A man is tested by the praise accorded him" (Prov. 27:21). God will test our desire to worship by allowing others to praise us. In those moments we can either begin to build an altar to the god of prestige, or we can take that praise and lift it up to the worthy One.

For many years the Midianites plundered the children of Israel. Then one day God called a man to lead the children of Israel out of that terrible situation. God told that man, Gideon, that he was a valiant warrior and that he would be used mightily. But there were two things Gideon must do first. One was to build an altar of worship. This Gideon did. After his encounter with the angel of the Lord Gideon built an altar that he called "The Lord is Peace." Worship was the result of his encounter with God.

The second was to tear down the altars to Baal. This Gideon also did. After the altars to the false gods were torn down, the Spirit of God came upon Gideon, for the man God anoints with His spirit is the man who worships only at the altar of Jehovah.

If we are to see the glory of God in this generation, we must destroy the altars in our hearts to the gods of the age. There must be room to worship only the lovely Lord Jesus. A. W. Tozer said, "If there is to be true and blessed worship, some things in your life must be destroyed, eliminated. The Gospel of Jesus Christ is certainly positive and constructive. But it must be destructive in some areas, dealing with and destroying certain elements that cannot remain in a life pleasing to God."[3]

NOTES

1. James Sterbe, "Mosque and State," *Wall Street Journal*, Aug. 13, 1987, p. 1.
2. Ibid., p. 14.
3. A. W. Tozer, *What Happened to Worship* (Camp Hill, Pa: Christian Pubns., 1985), p. 125.

No worship is wholly pleasing to God until there is nothing in me displeasing to God.

A. W. Tozer, *Whatever Happened to Worship*

Who may ascend into the hill of the Lord? Who may stand in His holy place? He who has clean hands and a pure heart, who has not lifted up his soul to falsehood, and has not sworn deceitfully.

Psalm 24:3-4

5
Worship in Spirit

I have met people from many of the great world religions. It has been interesting to note the difference in the principles of Christian worship and the worship of other religious groups. At first glance their worship appears to be very similar. But upon examination, it is clear that it is quite different. The foundation of Christian worship is God's grace. The foundation of the worship of the great world religions is performance. Christian worship begins with God. Religion begins with the efforts of man. Christianity is God reaching down to man. Religion is man's attempt to reach up to God.

Islam, for example, is an Arabic word that can be translated to mean "submission" or "surrender." For a Muslim the means of achieving a relationship with God is through surrender to the will of God. That sounds very good. Surrender and submission are words that are also very dear to the Christian. But there is a gap between Islamic worship and Christian worship that is as great as the difference between light and darkness.

CONTRAST OF CHRISTIAN WORSHIP TO OTHER RELIGIONS

In order to understand that difference, we must understand the nature of man. God created man in His own image. There are three aspects of the nature of God, but there is only one God. Even though we acknowledge the Father, the Son, and the Holy Spirit, the three are one. The Trinity is a difficult concept to comprehend, but it has helped me to realize that man is very similar to God because he was created in God's image.

There are three dimensions to our lives—the spiritual, the personality, and the physical. The spiritual dimension is the area where real worship originates. It is in the innermost part of our being. The dimension of the personality includes the will, mind, and emotions. The physical dimension is the outward part of our lives, and it functions primarily through our five senses.

The deepest dimension is the spiritual. This is the place where we commune with God. However, the spirit of man is dead because of sin. The Scripture says that "the wages of sin is death" (Rom. 6:23). Death does not mean annihilation; it means separation. The Greek scholar W. E. Vines says that death is "the separation of man from God. Adam died on the day he disobeyed God and hence all mankind are born in the same spiritual condition. Death is the opposite of life; it never denotes non-existence. As spiritual life is conscious existence in communion with God; so spiritual death is 'conscious existence in separation from God.' "[1]

Thus, man is separated from God in the deepest part of his being. There is a God-shaped vacuum deep within him. He was created to know, love, and worship God, but sin created a great gulf between himself and God. The question remains, "How then can we love and worship God when we are separated from Him?"

The diagram on the next page can help us to understand the dilemma of man.

The spirit of man is dead because of sin's effect on the human heart: man is separated from God. The key to restoring our relationship with God is the will. We don't "fall into sin." We choose to sin. With the exception of Jesus, every person since Adam has chosen to go his own way, to live apart from God. Jesus is the only man whose entire life could be described by His prayer, "Not My will, but Thine be done" (Luke 22:42). Jesus is the only man who lived a life

MAN IS SPIRITUALLY DEAD

PERSONALITY OF MAN

1. **WILL.**
   Man has sinned. He is
   a slave to sin. His will
   is closed to God.

2. **INTELLECT.**
   Affected by sin.

3. **EMOTIONS.**
   Affected by sin.

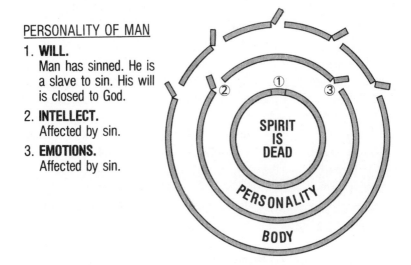

in which His will was surrendered 100 percent to the will of
God.

The best efforts of all of the rest of mankind fall pitifully
short of the mark of God's holiness and purity. The will of
every human is in bondage. Many of our best efforts to do
right are not for the glory of God, but for our own selfish
motives. Before I became a Christian, I was involved in civic
affairs and attempts to build a moral society. However, at
the center of all of my efforts was a desire for recognition. It
was not for the glorification of God that I served others. It
was for the gratification of my own ego. Yet this is true of all
people in all times. The will is in bondage to ego gratification.

Religion recognizes this problem. It tells people that
they must be submissive to a holy God, or they cannot really
love and worship Him. In that religion is partially correct—it
has diagnosed the problem of humanity, the need for submission to God. But religion is powerless to produce a will

that submits to the will of God solely for the purpose of glorifying God.

Instead, religion is built upon human performance. It attempts to make people right with God from the outside. It establishes a system of outward works designed to lead to true worship. It tells men that they must observe outward rituals and perform acts of goodness. If they do the right things, religion tells men, ultimately the mind and the emotions will achieve a state of tranquillity—and thus they will be able to worship God.

But man cannot live up to the outward standards of religion. The will remains a slave to sin, and the spiritual dimension of man is void of the Spirit of God. When man realizes his inability to meet the standards, religion leaves him frustated, empty, and judgmental. He has not achieved the fulfillment he had sought.

THE CHARACTER OF TRUE WORSHIP

True Christian worship does not originate from the outside. It originates from the innermost part of our being. True worship springs forth from the heart that has been graced by God. In order for there to be true worship there must be a spiritual rebirth in the innermost part of our lives. Jesus said, "God is spirit and those who worship Him must worship in spirit and truth" (John 4:24).

A very religious man came to Jesus one night. His name was Nicodemus, and he was a ruler among the Jewish people. Outwardly he was very religious. He knew that there was something unique about Jesus, and he came with questions about the true nature of Jesus. Nicodemus was shocked, however, when Jesus told him that he had to have a new birth in order to enter the kingdom of God. God's kingdom is spiritual, and worship in His kingdom must be spiritual worship. True worship in the kingdom of God cannot be accomplished by the outward keeping of the religious law. True worship must come from within. For that reason,

Jesus told Nicodemus, "That which is born of the flesh is flesh, and that which is born of the Spirit is spirit. Do not marvel that I said to you, 'You must be born again' " (John 3:6-7).

A person can be born of the Spirit only by the grace of God. We cannot physically, psychologically, or emotionally work our way into a spiritual birth. We must be born from above. Spiritual birth takes place in our hearts the moment the Spirit of God opens our hearts to the truth of the Son of God. The Spirit will bring events and people into our lives to show us the loveliness of the Lord Jesus. As we respond in faith, we are born from above; we are born of the Spirit of God.

Immediately we have the ability for true worship because we have the capacity to worship in spirit. Jesus said, "He who believes in Me, as the Scripture said, 'From his innermost being shall flow rivers of living water' " (John 7:38). John continued to explain the words of Jesus by writing, "But this He spoke of the Spirit, whom those who believed in Him were to receive; for the Spirit was not yet given, because Jesus was not yet glorified" (John 7:39).

After Jesus was crucified, buried, and raised from the tomb on the third day, He ascended to the right hand of the Father. It was then that He was glorified. Every corner of the universe cried out with the glory of Jesus. It was then that Jesus poured out His Spirit upon those who believed in Him. The Spirit of God came to dwell in the innermost part of the believers. And worship of Jesus flowed out of their lives as rivers of living water. They had received the capacity for true worship. They could worship in spirit because they had been born of the Spirit of God.

Contrast of Religious and Christian Worship

Herein lies the great difference between religious worship and true Christian worship: Religious worship originates in the flesh, or in the outer man. Christian worship

RELIGIOUS WORSHIP

- Originates from without.
- Appeals to the physical senses.

WILL IS CLOSED AND IN BONDAGE TO SIN

SPIRIT
IS
DEAD

CHRISTIAN WORSHIP

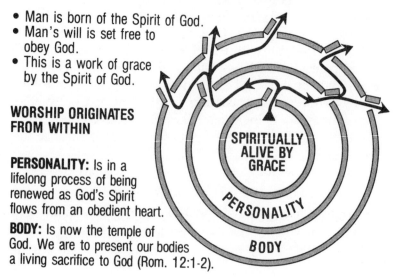

- Man is born of the Spirit of God.
- Man's will is set free to obey God.
- This is a work of grace by the Spirit of God.

WORSHIP ORIGINATES FROM WITHIN

PERSONALITY: Is in a lifelong process of being renewed as God's Spirit flows from an obedient heart.

BODY: Is now the temple of God. We are to present our bodies a living sacrifice to God (Rom. 12:1-2).

SPIRITUALLY
ALIVE BY
GRACE

PERSONALITY

BODY

originates in the Spirit, or in the innermost man. Religious worship is based on human performance. Christian worship is a work of the grace of God in the heart of man. Religious worship attempts to build an inward relationship with God by outward works. Christian worship is a result of an inward relationship with God where the Spirit of God freely flows outward, producing works of God's righteousness. Religious worship honors the worshiper. Christian worship honors the One worshiped. Religious worship compares itself to the worship of others. Christian worship sees only the glory of Jesus.

True worship then is the "supernaturally" natural flow of the Spirit of God through our entire being. The Holy Spirit is released from our innermost being because of the freedom of the will. The will of man has now been opened to the will of God.

The human will is probably the most important area of our lives in relation to the flow of spiritual worship from our hearts. The will of man is liberated to love, worship, and obey Jesus Christ. There are two things, however, that this new freedom does not mean. First, it does not mean that we have a license to sin. Quite the opposite. It means that we have been given freedom from the power and bondage of sin. Second, it does not mean that we are now perfect, that we will never again choose to do wrong. It means that we now have the power and ability to choose that which is right and to glorify God. We are no longer slaves who are mastered and controlled by ego gratification. Now we can freely choose to glorify God. But we must make that choice day by day and moment by moment.

CHRISTIANS CAN WORSHIP RELIGIOUSLY OR SPIRITUALLY: IT IS A PERSONAL CHOICE

Many Christians have tasted the joy of spiritual worship. Yet since that time they have lost the freshness of their worship. Much worship today among Christians is religious but not spiritual. The worshiper goes through the outward motions of worship but has lost the free flow of the Spirit of God through his life.

Recently when my wife and I were on the way to church we had a disagreement, and I spoke harshly to her. I knew that I had blocked the flow of God's Spirit in my life. There was a sense of grieving deep within me. Yet I was unrepentant. When we arrived at church, I tried to worship, but I was miserable. I had difficulty focusing on the loveliness of the Lord Jesus. Every time I attempted to look to Jesus, the Holy Spirit convicted me of my sin.

I had a choice to make. I could repent and restore my fellowship with God and my wife, or I could fake worship. I did the latter. I had a reputation to maintain. I was an international evangelist and Christian author. How would it look for someone in my position to go to the altar in repentance? I sang all the songs, said the "amens," and smiled and greeted all of my Christian friends. However, I did not worship Jesus Christ. I went through the outward motions, but I did not worship in spirit. True worship was not restored to my life until I made things right with God and my wife. It was only then that I was able to experience the joy of worship that originated from the release of the Spirit of God in my life.

RESULTS OF A CHOICE FOR RELIGIOUS WORSHIP

I am afraid that many Christians experience the same ritualistic worship that I did before I repented. Many have gone for years without a freshness in their love and worship of Jesus Christ. When this spiritual dryness occurs, and a person attempts to worship in spite of unconfessed sin in his life, normally one of three things happens.

⁓ Some persons continue to have their quiet times and go to church. But they have ceased to worship from rivers of living waters. They stand and worship at the banks of dried up river beds. They go through the outward motions religiously and with great discipline. But there is no genuine, living, joyful worship of Jesus.

The second group attempts to manipulate their worship experience. They try to stimulate the intellect or the emotions by outward displays of worship. If they belong to a church that is highly organized, they thrust themselves into great labors "for the Lord." These persons are often the ones who experience "burn out" in the church. Or if they are in a church that is more spontaneous in its style of worship, they might be the ones most moved emotionally. They have mountaintop religious experiences continually but never learn to walk in the valley. They have not yet learned the truth of the words of Jesus, "Blessed are the pure in heart for they shall see God" (Matt. 5:8).

The third group drops out altogether. There is no real joy or peace in their worship. As a consquence, they begin to criticize others. They blame everyone else for the lack of quality of worship. The preaching is too long, the music is too loud, they are too busy for a quiet time—it is always someone else's fault. Eventually they get tired of being miserable in church and quit attending. Or they become wearied by a boring quiet time and stop having time alone with God.

These three groups make up an enormous number of Christians in worship services today who are not experiencing Christian worship. They are worshiping according to the principles of religion rather than the principles of genuine spiritual worship. The apostle Paul wrote to Christians in Galatia dealing with this same problem. He asked them, "Are you so foolish? Having begun by the Spirit, are you being perfected by the flesh?" (Gal.3:3). It is a foolish thing to think that we can continue to grow in our worship of Jesus only by outward forms, rituals, and methods.

TESTING THE SPIRITUALITY OF WORSHIP

There are many styles and outward forms of worship within the Christian church. Many times we attempt to test the spirituality of worship by the quality of its outward form. Some think that spiritual worship is spontaneous in nature. Others think that it should be highly organized and very disciplined. Some feel that spiritual worship should be characterized by loud shouts of "Amen." Others think that true worship is quiet and meditative. Some like to lift up their hands. Others find that distractive. However, I have met people in each of these categories who are deeply spiritual in their worship of Jesus Christ. And I have met others in each category who are merely performing a religious duty of worship.

True worship cannot be defined as traditional or non-traditional. It is even possible to be traditional about our non-traditionalism. Tradition has to do with the repetition of a pattern, not with the essential character of the pattern. The key to true worship is not in the externals. It is in the purity of our hearts. The worship of Jesus Christ must never become so familiar that we simply go through the motions. Jesus is the One worthy of a pure heart and devotion in our worship.

During the revival of the Hebrides Islands in the 1950s many believers committed themselves to Psalm 24, an expression of God's directive for worship. The psalmist begins with a question, "Who may ascend into the hill of the Lord? And who may stand in His holy place?" (Ps. 24:3). He answers that question by saying that for a man or a woman to be a true worshiper he or she must meet three requirements. First, that person must have clean hands. Our hands are the most likely parts of our bodies to pick up disease as we go into the world. A Romanian medical doctor often interprets for me when I preach in his country. At the conclusion of the services, we greet the people and shake hundreds of hands. He then always tells me, "Sammy, before we do anything else, we need to have clean hands."

The same is true in our spiritual walk in the world. The world is full of a spiritual disease called sin. Before we come to the place of worship, we must have clean hands. We must right all wrongs and confess all sins. We must see the necessity and urgency of being clean before God. We must not wait until we hear an inspiring sermon. Worship does not take place only between 11:00 and 12:00 on Sunday mornings. Worship transpires daily. Therefore we must not allow any spiritual disease in this world to attach itself to our lives. If we are to stand before the Lord in worship, we must come with clean hands.

Second, the psalmist says that we must have a pure heart. The test of worship becomes more difficult at this point. Not only must we keep our lives clean in our outward relationship to the world around us, but we must keep our inner lives pure within us.

Purity of heart gives us clarity of vision to see God in His greatness and splendor. I recall the first time that I was told that I needed to wear glasses. I had lived for more than thirty years without ever knowing that I needed glasses. My defect was only a minor one, but when I put my glasses on for the first time, I couldn't believe it. I didn't know that the world could be so clear. I would drive down the street in my car constantly taking my glasses off and putting them on. I would chuckle and say, "This is great. The world is so much more beautiful than I could have ever imagined."

The same is true with the attitude of our hearts. Many Christians have harbored attitudes in their hearts for years that have kept them from seeing God clearly. Bitterness and guilt cloud our view of God. Other ungodly attitudes also cloud our vision of Him. If we are to worship Him in spirit, we must rid ourselves of all of the inward impurities in our lives.

Finally, the psalmist says that we must use our tongues to glorify God. The book of James says that the tongue may be small, but it is powerful. It can be the instrument to express worship to God, or it can be an instrument to curse people. If we expect God to accept the sacrifice of praise from our lips, we must be careful to allow our lips to be used only as an instrument of blessing.

How then can we stand in the place of true spiritual worship? Our whole lives must be yielded to the Holy Spirit by the grace of God. David said that the one who can truly stand in the place of worship is "he who has clean hands and a pure heart, who has not lifted up his soul to falsehood, and has not sworn deceitfully" (Psalm 24:4). That is the person who can stand in the place of worship.

NOTE

1. W. E. Vine, *Vine's Expository Dictionary of New Testament Words* (McLean, Va.: MacDonald), p. 278.

The only way in which it is possible for us to "feed on Christ" is through the Word of God. Simply to study the Bible from an intellectual standpoint in order to know it, is not to feed on Him; and, moreover, such study is not sufficient. On the other hand, to attempt to know Christ and to feed on Christ apart from the Bible is impossible because God has ordained that as the vehicle of His communication to man.

G. Campbell Morgan,
in *This Was His Faith*

God is spirit, and those who worship Him must worship Him in spirit and truth.

John 4:24

6
Worship in Truth

Throughout the ages, the light of the glory of God has burst into hearts of men and women through the ministry of the Word of God. Martin Luther read the Scriptures for the first time in an Augustinian monastery. His life would never be the same after meditating on the truth found in that Book. He discovered the wonder, glory, and loveliness of Jesus. The Book that Luther read would produce a Reformation of an entire society.

Anytime and anywhere people have discovered the truth of the Scriptures, it has resulted in a great awakening of their hearts to worship the Lord Jesus. It was preaching of the Bible that brought me into a personal and eternal relationship with God. It has been the constant study and meditation on the Scripture that has kept a freshness in my love relationship with the Savior. Every day I am able to discover some jewel in His character through the Word of God.

My first pastorate was at the Hahn Baptist Church in Hahn, West Germany. A wise old pastor encouraged me to preach expositorily verse by verse through the Bible. I accepted his encouragement and began preaching through the book of Genesis. It took me close to three years to preach completely through Genesis. I discovered during those years how great and awesome our God is. I also discovered that the Bible was food for the souls of the people. People filled the church. We had to move into the local high school because of lack of space in the church facilities. Worship services became exciting. People came with hearts hungry to learn more of the Savior.

Something dynamic happens when the Bible is opened. Lives are changed. Christ is exalted. And worship flows from the hearts of God's people. The miracle that transpires in the hearts of people is inexplicable.

Several years ago I was a guest on a talk program at a Chicago television station with five other ministers from various religious backgrounds. The host was an agnostic. Four of the ministers did not believe the Bible was the infallible, inspired Word of God, although three of the four were from Christian denominational churches. Only two of us accepted the Bible as God's holy, infallible, inspired communication to mankind. After much debate regarding the inspiration of the Scripture, the agnostic television host stated, "I tend to agree with you gentlemen who don't hold to the absolute reliability of the Scriptures. But there is one thing that really bothers me. Why is it that the churches that preach the Bible are all filled? Why are people leaving the churches that don't emphasize the Bible and flocking to the ones that are fundamentally teaching and preaching the Scriptures?"

The phenomenon he had noticed really is a mystery from a purely logical viewpoint. Why do people in an advanced, twentieth-century society live by an ancient Book written thousands of years ago by numerous authors? What is in that Book that has captured the loyalty of millions of people throughout the centuries? Why has that Book captivated the best intellects of the ages? Why did such great men as Saul of Tarsus, Ambrose, Augustine, John Calvin, Martin Luther, George Whitefield, John Wesley, and Jonathan Edwards give their entire lives to the preaching of that Book? Why would men and women be willing to be burned at the stake for the sake of the truth in that Book? Why do men and women today risk their future, their families, and even imprisonment to bring that Book to closed societies?

There is a simple but wonderful answer to all of these questions. That Book contains words of life for the souls of all people, from all generations, who have lived in every land. It is the testimony of the God who created them and the Savior who is able to redeem them and who offers them life abundant and eternal. It is the love letter from the One in whom we all have our existence. It is the testimony of Jesus.

A great spiritual awakening took place in Britain in the eighteenth century. There were numerous Christian leaders during that period of British history. Bishop J. C. Ryle said of those leaders that "in all their preaching they were eminently men of one book. To that book they were content to pin their faith, and by it to stand or fall. This was one grand characteristic of their preaching. They honored, they loved, they reverenced the Bible."[1]

One of those leaders was George Whitefield. He was a man of the Bible. He studied, memorized, loved, and preached the Bible. Thousands came to the open fields to hear Whitefield preach from the Book. At some points in his life he preached forty to fifty hours each week. And he always preached from that grand old Book. Early in his ministry he developed an intense love and desire to study the Bible. Arnold Dallimore in his biography of Whitefield describes a scene of a morning in the early life of Mr. Whitefield. He writes, "There he is at five in the morning, in the room above Harris book store. He is on his knees with his English Bible, his Greek New Testament and Henry's Commentary spread out before him. He reads a portion in the English, gains a fuller insight into it as he studies words and tenses in the Greek and then considers Matthew Henry's explanation of it all. Finally, there comes the unique practice that he has developed: that of 'praying over every line and word' of both the English and the Greek till the passage, in its essential message, veritably become part of his own soul."[2]

Whitefield became a mighty man of God during his generation because he learned intimately and accurately of the character of God described in the Bible. The Scriptures do not merely give us a fleeting acquaintance with God. They introduce us to an intimate knowledge of His great deeds and moral character and of the basic principles by which He governs the universe. Therefore, a true worshiper will be one who loves and delights in the Word of God.

The psalmist wrote an acrostic that emphasizes the importance of the Word of God in worship. That acrostic, Psalm 119, speaks of seven works of grace that the Word of God will produce in the heart of the one who worships according to its truth: purity of life, revival of the soul, strength and comfort of the afflicted, guidance and protection for the journey of life, joy in the spirit, understanding in our minds, deliverance from the bonds of sin.

Purity of Life

"How can a young man keep his way pure? By keeping it according to Thy word. . . . Thy word I have treasured in my heart, that I may not sin against Thee" (Ps. 119:9, 11). Purity of heart is the prerequisite for clarity in our vision of God. The psalmist therefore asks how a person can truly have a pure heart and life. The answer is quite simple.

The Word of God in us and lived out through us produces purity of life. It has the ability to cleanse us from everything that is unlike Christ. Jesus said, "You search the Scriptures, because you think that in them you have eternal life; and it is these that bear witness of Me" (John 5:39). They are the standard of God by which we measure ourselves. From Genesis to Revelation, they are the testimony of Jesus. He is our standard. When we read the Scriptures, we see how unlike Him we really are, which produces brokenness, repentance, and cleansing in our hearts. Then we are in a spiritual position to clearly see God and worship Him.

Revival of the Soul

"My soul cleaves to the dust; Revive me according to Thy word" (Ps. 119:25). Throughout the ages, the great revivals of Christianity have been directly related to the ministry of the Word of God. As wonderful as is music of praise, it will not produce a great spiritual or moral revival.

It is pleasant to have creative means of worship in our churches and personal lives. However, there is no substitute for the ministry of the Scriptures. They have the ability to revive the weak and sickly saint. They turn the focus of the Christian away from defeat and point him to the victory of the conquering Christ.

On many occasions in my personal walk with God, I have felt discouraged and defeated. But I only have to be still and meditate on the Scriptures to discover the One who is able to revive the heavy heart. The Scriptures have the ability to shine forth the glory of God in places where His light has grown dim. Spiritual renewal comes to the individual, church, or community that is open to the light of God's Word.

Strength and Comfort for the Afflicted

"My soul weeps because of grief; strengthen me according to Thy word. . . . O may Thy lovingkindness comfort me, according to Thy word to Thy servant" (Ps. 119:28, 76). John Wesley was a man of the Bible. He once said, "Oh, give me that book! At any price give me the book of God. . . . Let me be a man of one book."[3]

Why was that Book of such great importance to Wesley? For one thing, it gave great strength and comfort to him and to many of his followers during the most difficult times. Wesley also said, "Our people did well! The world may find fault with our opinions, but the world cannot deny that our people did well."[4] In other words, that Book not only gave Wesley the strength to live in the grace of God, but also to die in His grace. During the deepest times of sorrow Wesley found that the Bible pointed him to the true source of strength and comfort.

GUIDANCE AND PROTECTION FOR THE JOURNEY OF LIFE

"Thy Word is a lamp to my feet and a light to my path" (Ps. 119:105). The human heart desperately cries out with the need for security. People attempt to build their futures around two gifts in life that tend to make them feel secure.

First, they seek security in other people. The only problem is that all people have one tragic human flaw: sin. Sin causes the bottom to fall out of our security because sin brings death. Therefore, one day we will lose those who make us feel the most secure. Also, sin brings disappointment. Because of the fallen nature of humanity, our friends and family will eventually fail us. Absolute security cannot be found in people.

Second, people attempt to find security in material possessions. There is a tendency to think that nicer homes, bigger automobiles, and higher salaries will produce the kind of security that we need in our lives. However, after several years of observing people from all walks of life, I have drawn one conclusion: there is no industry or occupation that can guarantee security.

Why is it that people, positions, and possessions cannot give assurances of absolute security? They cannot predict the future. The Scriptures, however, introduce us to the God who is eternal. He existed before we were born and will live after we are dead. He knows every part of our genetic makeup. He is fully aware of our strengths and our weaknesses. He is not only fully knowledgeable of history, but history is really His story. He knows everything about everyone who has ever lived. And He holds the power to order the events of our lives. He can mold our destiny and mend our past.

The Word of God guides us to the path upon which this eternal, almighty, omniscient God desires us to walk. It is the light which directs us through the dark and dangerous times of life. It is the only place to find true security. The heart that has found its security in God will certainly be a worshiping heart.

Joy in the Spirit

"I rejoice at Thy word as one who finds great spoil" (Ps. 119:162). Many people think that they must be only solemn in their worship of God, that worship should carry with it only a sense of reverence and respect for the Creator. They are partly right—solemnity and respect for God are a part of worship. But in worship there should also be a deep sense of joy flowing from the heart that knows and worships God. The Word of God contains the treasures of God's glory. Each time we open the Scriptures with a pure heart, we will discover another jewel in the character of God. Those diamonds in His character will bring great delight to our hearts, which will result in joyful worship.

Understanding in Our Minds

"Let my cry come before Thee, O Lord; Give me understanding according to Thy word" (Ps. 119:169). Many people experience a shallowness in their worship because they do not correctly understand the nature of God. Others have given themselves to completely false worship because they have an incorrect basis for their faith.

Several years ago I was approached on the streets of Amsterdam by a group of young people witnessing. They were telling people that they needed to accept Christ into their hearts. They invited me to their "Christian coffee house." I was excited to meet what appeared to be vivacious young believers. However, the coffee house turned out to be a "Christian disco" where they "hustled people for Jesus."

I discussed in detail the claims of Christ with them. They told me that they believed that Allah is God, Mohammed His prophet, and Jesus His son. Obviously they did not draw those conclusions from the Bible. Yet they continually quoted verses of Scripture. I asked them how they could believe the Bible and claim to be followers of Mohammed at the same time. I discovered that there was a "great prophet" who was head of their group. This "prophet" had final authority in matters of their faith.

That was the same type of cultic following that Jim Jones gathered around himself. A great tragedy occurred because hundreds of people heeded the words of Jim Jones as their final authority rather than the Word of God. The final, authoritative revelation of God to man is not the Bible plus a prophet. Nor is it the Bible plus another great religious book. The final revelation of the person, attributes, and nature of God is found in the Bible alone. If we are to have a correct understanding of the moral character of God, we must become people of that one great Book, the Bible. Without the Holy Scriptures we may find ourselves worshiping a false god. Jesus said that true worshipers would not only worship in spirit but also in truth. The Word of God is absolute truth.

Deliverance from the Bonds of Sin

"Let my supplication come before Thee; Deliver me according to Thy word" (Ps. 119:170). The first song of worship recorded in the Bible is found in Exodus 15. The nation of Israel had lived in bondage to the Egyptians for four hundred years. They had been treated brutally. Then, after four hundred years of slavery, God worked miracles to deliver them from their captivity. Their worship of God must have been splendid at that time, because they had come to know Him as their Deliverer.

Some of the most moving moments of history have been the times in which people have been freed from their bondage. It must have been an awesome and inspiring moment when Jews were released from concentration camps at the end of World War II. Yet the greatest bondage known to humanity is mankind's slavery to sin. It is a bondage that is as old as Adam. People still battle slavery to immoral desires, hate, greed, drug abuse, and envy, just as they have for thousands of years. Man's will remains a slave to the destructive demands of sin.

But there is good news. And that "good news" is found in the Word of God. God's Word is able to liberate us from every spiritual and immoral prison in which our hearts are captured. Why does the Word of God have the power to liberate our hearts? First, the Bible is the written Word of God. Jesus is the living Word of God. The Bible simply points us to Jesus, who is the true Deliverer. Jesus said, "You shall know the truth, and the truth shall make you free" (John 8:32). He explained further by saying, "If therefore the Son shall make you free, you shall be free indeed" (John 8:36). Much of the earthly ministry of Jesus was to set the captive free. That ministry has never ceased.

Because the Bible is a testimony of Jesus, it has brought the message of deliverance to men and women for thousands of years. There was a young man who heard the Word of God in England during the mid-1800s. He described his experience years later when he said, "Personally, I have to bless God . . . not for good books but for the preached Word—and that too addressed to me by a poor, uneducated man, a man who had never received any training for the ministry, and probably will never be heard of in his life, a man engaged in business, no doubt of a humble kind, during the week, but who had just enough grace to say on the Sabbath, 'Look unto Me, and be ye saved, all the ends of the earth.' The revealed word awakened me, but it was the preached Word that saved me; and I must ever attach peculiar value to the hearing of the truth, for by it I received the joy and peace in which my soul delights."[5]

This young man gave his life to proclaiming the Word of God. Thousands found deliverance and salvation through his preaching. By the age of nineteen, there was not a building in London that could contain the people who came to hear this young man preach from that grand old Book. His name was Charles Haddon Spurgeon, and he never ceased to proclaim the greatness of the Savior from the Word of God.

When a person is set free from slavery to sin by the living Word of God as revealed in the written Word of God, he will always respond with joyful worship. That person will worship in truth because he has been set free by the One who is Truth.

If we are to worship in truth, the Bible must be the centerpiece of our worship experience. The Word of God from beginning to end will direct us to Jesus, the One worthy of our worship.

Notes

1. J. C. Ryle, *Christian Leaders of the 18th Century* (Edinburgh: Banner of Truth, 1985), p. 26.
2. Arnold Dallimore, *George Whitefield* (Westchester, Ill.: Cornerstone, 1970), 1:82-83.
3. J. C. Ryle, *Christian Leaders of the 18th Century*, p. 90.
4. Ibid., p. 173.
5. C. H. Spurgeon, *Autobiography* (Edinburgh: Banner of Truth, 1976), 1:86.

At the martyrdom of Faustines and Jovita, brothers and citizens of Brescia, their torments were so many, and their patience so great, that Calocerius, a pagan, beholding them, was struck with admiration, and exclaimed in a kind of ecstasy, Great is the God of the Christians! for which he was apprehended, and suffered a similar fate.

Fox's Book of Martyrs

But to the degree that you share the sufferings of Christ, keep on rejoicing; so that also at the revelation of His glory, you may rejoice with exultation. If you are reviled for the name of Christ, you are blessed, because the Spirit of glory and of God rests upon you.

1 Peter 4:13-14

7

Suffering and Worship

It is quite common in this generation to hear glowing testimonies of Christians who speak of a life without pain and sorrow. Many such testimonies tell of difficulties before the speaker came to know Christ. But after becoming a Christian the individual seemingly has no problems. Life is just a "bed of roses."

I seriously doubt the accuracy of such testimonies. Christians throughout the generations have encountered more difficulties after their conversions than before they came to Christ. Christianity is not the absence of hardship or suffering in life. It is the glory and grace of God in the heart of the hurting believer. A Christian receives no exemption from the hurts of humanity. It is often in the midst of suffering that the Christian learns to worship Jesus Christ. He learns to appreciate and adore Him as he gains a greater understanding of Christ's suffering. It is in the trying circumstances that his understanding of God's love is deepened.

Early in our marriage, my wife and I moved to a ghetto area of Chicago. We ministered to drug addicts, runaways, and street gangs. We witnessed and shared Christ on the streets in one of the most difficult areas of Chicago. God blessed the ministry, and many young people came to know Jesus. We held follow-up Bible studies for the new believers.

As we realized the possibility of impacting Chicago for Christ, we began praying for a mighty spiritual awakening within the city. We passed out gospel pamphlets each evening in a nightclub district and shared Christ with anyone who would listen. We couldn't believe the results. The clubs would normally close at 4:00 A.M. each morning. But our witnessing on the streets began to make its impact on the clubs. They had to close at midnight because of the lack of business.

The owners of the nightclubs were enraged. They did everything they could to remove us from the streets. They threatened, embarrassed, and ridiculed us. Lloyd Cole, a co-worker, and I were passing out our pamphlets one evening, and I spoke with a man who wanted to know Christ. He told me, "I don't know why I come to these places. My life is a mess. I need Christ." We knelt on the sidewalk and he invited Christ into his life. Instead of going into the club, he went home.

The barker in front of the nightclub got angry. He pulled out a knife and threatened to stab me. Not long after the encounter with the barker, two plainclothes policemen came out of the club. We told them of the threat from the club barker. We could not believe what happened next. They "read us our rights" and placed us under arrest. We were taken to the city jail and booked for disorderly conduct. The charges stated that there were "three or more persons inciting a riotous situation."

I couldn't believe it! There were only two of us, and we were quietly sharing our faith on the streets. I couldn't believe that such an arrest could actually take place in America. We were allowed one telephone call. I called my wife, Tex, who was close to nine months pregnant with our first child. Lloyd and I were placed in a cell, surrounded by drunks and common criminals. The officers confiscated our Bibles.

Before I became a Christian, I was president of the Baton Rouge Junior Rotarians and president of the East Baton Rouge Parish Youth Council. I was the author of a proclamation for "Patriotism Day" in my home city, which was signed into effect by our mayor. I was one of thirty students to represent my state in a study at the United Nations. There I was awarded "Outstanding Youth Speaker" in North America. I had earned the respect of my friends, community, and government. But now I was in jail. I was being treated like a common criminal for one reason: I had found the love of the Savior, and I simply wanted others to know that love.

Lloyd and I sat in our jail cell in utter disbelief. But we came to love and appreciate Jesus that evening to a degree that we had never before known. Two things happened in my heart. First, I received a glimpse of the love of the Savior. I realized that He had been falsely accused. He did wrong to no one. Yet He was despised, rejected, and crucified. But He loved us in the midst of His suffering. In my suffering I began to appreciate His suffering. In my rejection I discovered His acceptance.

Second, Jesus made my heart tender toward those who suffer for His sake. Much of my ministry today is in areas of the world where it is unpopular to be a Christian. I travel often to areas of the world where Christians suffer for their faith. That evening in jail God placed a special love in my heart for the Christians who face great difficulties because of their love for Jesus. A direction was set for my life in that cell. I could know the hurt of human abuse and the comfort of God in the midst of that abuse. My heart was softened toward those who suffer for His name's sake.

But most of all, I learned to worship in the midst of difficulty. Lloyd and I felt so alone in that cell. We looked at each other and I asked, "What do we do now?"

We began to pray, then sing. We began worshiping God in jail. Our bodies were kept in cages like animals, but our spirits soared freely. We sang, "Amazing grace, how sweet the sound that saved a wretch like me." At first the other prisoners were yelling at us. But then one of them asked, "If you are Christians, then why are you in jail?"

We explained what had transpired that evening. It gave us a golden opportunity to preach the gospel. A man in the cell next to us said, "I stabbed a man tonight. Is there any hope for me? I need God." We led him in a prayer of repentance and faith in Christ. How we began to worship in that lonely jail cell!

Later that evening my wife bailed us out of jail. It was very humiliating. Before I became a Christian, I was an upstanding, well-respected citizen. Now I had to be bailed out of jail by my wife because I had shared Christ on the streets.

God turned humiliation into an opportunity to proclaim the glory of Jesus to hundreds of thousands of people. I built a cross and placed it across the street from the office of the late Mayor Richard J. Daley, Chicago's longtime mayor. I stayed there, praying and fasting until my trial. Every major newspaper in Chicago carried stories of our plight. I was able to share Christ with the city. Secular radio and television stations continually interviewed me. One major television station had a thirty-minute segment given totally to informing the public about our situation. It allowed people throughout the city to ask me any question about myself or my arrest that they wanted to ask. The program gave me a wonderful opportunity to share what Christ had done in my life.

Many Christians throughout the nation supported us. Letters of protest were sent to the city of Chicago from churches, political leaders, and individual Christians. It was overwhelming. The morning that I awakened to go to trial, my wife went into labor. When I left to go to court, she was being rushed to the hospital to have our first child. It is impossible to describe the emotions I felt that day. Eventually the city of Chicago admitted to false arrest and dropped the charges. Lloyd and I signed papers saying that we would not sue the city. And my son, Dave, was born on the day that I went to trial for telling people on the streets about Jesus.

In the midst of my difficulties with the city of Chicago, God taught me three important lessons about worship and its relationship to suffering. The most beautiful moments of worship are often experienced during the deepest and darkest days of difficulty. Therefore, it is extremely important that we allow the suffering and pain in our lives to transform shallow, empty worship into deep, meaningful experiences of adoration for the Savior.

I do not understand suffering; it is a great mystery to me. I don't fully understand why the righteous suffer. I don't understand why a city arrested two young men who were helping drug addicts and alcoholics to find a new life in Christ. I don't understand why my best friend met tragic death in an automobile accident in the prime of his life. I don't understand why my father suffered with a rare disease for ten years and then died while I was at the university. There are many things concerning suffering that are beyond my comprehension. I don't know the answer to "why." But I do know "what" suffering has produced in my life. It has caused me to look deep into my soul and by faith to lay hold of the grace of God. It has brought me into a deeper and more intimate knowledge of Him.

FRUIT OF SUFFERING

Suffering can produce a deeper experience of worship because it deepens the character of the one who worships. Suffering is often the training ground for godly character. It has a way of exposing what is shallow and superficial in our lives. Suffering begins to burn away superficiality the moment the match of difficulty is lit and set among the embers of the events of our lives.

There is a second fruit of the suffering that touches our lives. It not only produces character within us that is capable of meaningful worship, but it also broadens our ministry of worship. Worship of Jesus Christ should be contagious. The book of Exodus gives an account of the worship of Moses. He pitched his tent outside the camp away from the multitudes of people. There he met with God and worshiped Him. He called it the "tent of the meeting." He met with God and spoke with Him, and God spoke with Moses. It is interesting to note what happened in the lives of the people when Moses met with God. The Bible says, "When all the people saw the pillar of the cloud standing at the entrance of the tent, all the people would arise and worship, each at the entrance of the tent" (Exodus 33:10). When Moses worshiped God, the people worshiped God.

True worship will always attract a crowd. The congregation of Christians that has learned to worship from the depths of their hearts will attract people, because worship of God is one of the most basic needs of humanity. The individual who truly worships God will have opportunities to lead others to worship Him.

This is especially true among those who have suffered. The apostle Paul wrote, "Blessed be the God and Father of our Lord Jesus Christ, the Father of mercies and God of all comfort; who comforts us in all our affliction so that we may be able to comfort those who are in any affliction with the comfort with which we ourselves are comforted by God" (2 Cor. 1:3-4).

Christians have suffered throughout the ages. But suffering has always been the friend of the believer—not the enemy. The early church was persecuted. Every time a Christian was killed, it seemed as though there were ten new converts to Christianity. Suffering always tests the fabric of a person's worship. It brings out the worst or the best in the hearts of believers. When there is true, humble worship of God in the heart, there is an inward beauty that is inexplicable. Others will be attracted to worship the Savior.

Aside from the Bible, *Pilgrim's Progress* has been perhaps the best selling Christian book of all time. Its author, John Bunyan, was a man who suffered greatly for his faith. Through his suffering he encountered God in a sweet experience of worship. And he became a source of inspiration to scores of people throughout the world. He wrote concerning his imprisonment for preaching, "Before I went down to the justice, I begged of God that His will be done; for I was not without hopes that my imprisonment might be an awakening to the saints in the country. Only in that matter did I commit the thing to God. And verily at my return I did meet my God sweetly in prison."[1]

There seems to be a direct correlation between suffering, worship, and witness. Suffering deepens the experience of worship, and genuine worship broadens the witness of the Christian community. Friends of mine from the West who have traveled with me to Romania have made some interesting observations. One of those friends said to me, "I have always heard of the Christians who suffer for their faith in Romania. I think that the suffering has produced a quality of worship and witness of which we in the West know very little. It seems as though the comfortable Christian in the West is really the one who is suffering. We suffer from the disease of superficiality in our worship and witness."

A final fruit of worship is produced in the individual who suffers. Suffering is accompanied by the glory of God. The final result of worship is the glory of God. It is wonderful that character is built through the struggles and hurts of life. It is even greater that we are able to comfort others as a result of our suffering. However, the single greatest goal of the life of the believer should be the glory of God, who is worthy of all the glory and all the honor and worship. Peter said, "If you are reviled for the name of Christ, you are blessed, because the Spirit of glory and of God rests upon you" (1 Peter 4:13).

Death is the final blow of suffering. It can't get worse than that. But death cannot conquer the child of God. Death for the believer is simply graduation day from the school of worship. Billy Bray, whose life of worship we discussed in chapter 1, faced life's ultimate test—death. A few hours before he died, an old friend asked him if he had any fear of death, or of being lost. He responded, "What? Me fear death? Me, lost? Why, my Savior conquered death. If I were to go down to hell, I would shout glory, glory, to my blessed Jesus, until I made the bottomless pit ring again, and then miserable old Satan would say, 'Billy, Billy, this is no place for thee: get thee back.' Then up to heaven I should go, shouting, glory, glory, praise the Lord!"[2] A little later he passed into eternity. The last word to come from his lips on this earth was simply, "Glory!"

From the time of the first Christian martyr, Stephen, to the present day, Christians have worshiped God and beheld His glory during the difficult day of death. The Bible describes the moments prior to the death of Stephen, "But being full of the Holy Spirit, he gazed intently into heaven and saw the glory of God, and Jesus standing at the right hand of God; and he said, 'Behold, I see the heavens opened up and the Son of Man standing at the right hand of God' " (Acts 7:55-56).

Throughout the centuries worshiping saints have seen the glory of God when they approached death's door. The great American evangelist Dwight L. Moody said on the afternoon of his death, "God is calling me. There's no pain. No valley. This is glorious."[3] More recently, Martin Lloyd-Jones, the great British pastor, walked up to death's door. The day before he died he told his family, "Don't pray for healing. Don't try to hold me back from glory."[4] He died the next day peacefully in his sleep.

Suffering can be a friend to the one who has learned to worship. There is no hurt physically, psychologically, emotionally, or spiritually that God does not understand. He loves us greatly and He suffered greatly for us through the death of His Son, Jesus. When a true worshiper suffers, the door to the glory of God is opened to him. He enters into the fellowship of the sufferings of Christ. It is then that he is able to comprehend more fully the heighth and depth and breadth and width of the love of God. He learns to worship the worthy One in the midst of suffering.

Notes

1. *Foxe's Book of Martyrs* (Grand Rapids, Mich.: Zondervan, 1967), p. 328.
2. F. W. Bourne, *The Life of Billy Bray* (Monmouth, Gwent, U.K.: Bridge, 1987), pp. 85-86.
3. Faith Bailey, *D. L. Moody* (Chicago: Moody, 1959), p. 158.
4. Ian Barclay, *Death and the Life to Come* (London: Hodder & Stoughton, 1988), p. 66.

The Devil hates music because he cannot stand gaiety. . . . Satan can smirk but he cannot laugh, he can sneer but cannot sing.

Martin Luther, in
The Stories Behind
Great Hymns

Sing for joy in the Lord, O you righteous ones; Praise is becoming to the upright. Give thanks to the Lord with the lyre; sing praises to Him with a harp of ten strings. Sing to Him a new song; Play skillfully with a shout of joy.

Psalm 33:1-3

8
Song of Worship

Several years ago I was in a Romanian church near the Soviet border. I was scheduled to preach immediately after a musical presentation by a youth orchestra. The young people had formed a string orchestra consisting primarily of violins, guitars, and mandolins. They began to play some of the grand old hymns of the Christian faith. My heart was thrilled as they played and sang about the great attributes of our God. I imagine that heaven must be similar to that experience of worship. I wanted to shout. I wanted to cry. Instead, I just sat there in silence, worshiping the Savior.

Since that time, I have traveled often throughout Romania. But one factor concerning those youth groups always puzzled me: the high percentage of young people who played musical instruments. In some congregations I discovered that 100 percent of the youth played a musical instrument. Everywhere I have gone in Romania, I have discovered youth orchestras and choirs that really worshiped God through their music.

I asked a friend of mine if all young people were required by the schools to learn to play a musical instrument. He responded, "Oh, no. This phenomenon is a result of the 'new evangelical-Protestant revival' within the country. Where the Spirit of God is deeply at work and people are coming to Christ," he said, "young people are learning musical skills and singing a new song unto the Lord."

As I thought about it, I realized this occurrence has been true for centuries. When people encounter God, a melody in the heart is always produced, which must have an outward expression. True worship demands a medium for expression of love and adoration to God for His goodness and greatness. When the children of Israel were delivered by God from their hundreds of years of slavery, worship and praise flowed from their hearts in song. Later, David sang unto the Lord about His great deeds and amazing attributes. In the New Testament, Paul spoke to the Christians whose lives were controlled by the Holy Spirit, saying, "[speak] to one another in psalms and hymns and spiritual songs, singing and making melody with your heart" (Ephesians 5:19).

Many of the great hymns were written because men and women encountered our great God. Their music was simply a vehicle to transport to heaven what was in their hearts. They created music with joy and thanksgiving for the goodness of God.

One such great poet and hymnist was William Cowper, who lived from 1731 to 1800. When he was only six years old, his heart was broken as a result of his mother's death. He attended a boarding school and more suffering was added to his already hurting heart by the cruelty of some of the other boys. Cowper was depressed because he felt a deep sense of unworthiness. He attempted suicide several times, had two unhappy love affairs, and lived with a sense of inferiority.

For a brief period of time he was placed in an asylum. It was there that he met God. A relative visited him and shared with him from the Scriptures: "Whom God hath set forth to be a propitiation through faith in his blood" (Rom. 3:25 KJV). The relative shared with Cowper the gospel of Jesus Christ. He responded in faith and later testified, "It was the first time that I have seen a ray of hope. . . . There shone upon me the full beams of the sufficiency of the atonement that Christ has made; my pardon in His blood; the fulness and completeness of my justification and, in a moment, I believed and received the gospel."[1]

It was in that asylum that he wrote the great hymn, "There is a fountain filled with blood, drawn from Immanuel's veins; and sinners plunged beneath that flood, lose all their guilty stains." Cowper was simply a sinner who needed a Savior. When Jesus found him, melody replaced misery, and music transported his worship to the throne of God. His sense of depression was transformed into a sense of personal dignity by the One worthy of worship.

When I came to know Christ as a freshman in the university, two very interesting changes occurred in my life. I immediately fell in love with books. Prior to coming to know Christ, I read very little. Reading had been a chore to me; I read only what my teachers assigned in class. But when I came to Christ, I began to devour the Bible. It was bread from heaven to my heart. I wasn't reading in order to get a good grade in school. The Bible was a heavenly love letter that could only be understood in the realm of the heart. For years my heart had been closed. When I met Christ, my heart was opened to His love, and the Bible became exciting. I also began reading the biographies of the great Christian leaders of past centuries. Christian literature took on an important role in my life.

The second transformation in my heart was a love for a new kind of music. Because I had met Jesus, the Lover of my soul, I wanted to sing a new song unto Him. I probably rank among the worst singers in the world; my music can be distracting to those around me because I just do not have any natural musical abilities. But it is a sweet sound to the heart of the heavenly Father. When Jesus came into my life, a new song exploded in my heart. It was a song of worship and adoration.

CHARACTERISTICS OF MUSIC IN WORSHIP

There are three primary characteristics of music in relation to worship. First, it affords the Christian a response to the biblical revelation of God. A thorough study of the great hymns of the Christian faith will guide us to men and women who had a glimpse of the character of God. The blind hymnist, Fanny Crosby, understood the greatness of God and wrote, "To God be the glory! Great things He hath done." Edward Perronet came to Christ through the ministry of John Wesley. He grew in his faith and saw Jesus as the King of the universe. He responded by writing, "All hail the power of Jesus' name! Let angels prostrate fall; Bring forth the royal diadem and crown Him Lord of all."

Martin Luther's Reformation faced severe opposition. During those days, Luther often meditated on Psalm 46:1, "God is our refuge and strength, a very present help in trouble." Out of this knowledge of God as his refuge he wrote, "Ein feste Burg ist unser Gott," or in English, "A mighty fortress is our God." It was the song of the common man of the Reformation and inspiration to the martyrs for Christ.

John Newton almost lost his life in a terrible storm off the coast of northwest Ireland. He cried to God for mercy, and God saved him. He came to know God as the God of grace and mercy. He wrote, "Amazing grace! how sweet the sound, that saved a wretch like me! I once was lost, but now am found, was blind, but now I see." And Bishop Reginald Heber, an Anglican clergyman, was awakened to the absolute purity of God and wrote, "Holy, holy, holy, Lord God Almighty! Early in the morning our song shall rise to Thee; Holy, Holy, Holy! Merciful and Mighty! God in three Persons, blessed Trinity!"

But music is far more than a response to a revelation of God's attributes. It is also an expression of worship and thanksgiving for the transformed life that an encounter with God produces. It is a means of testimony to the works of God in the heart of man. The miraculous birth, perfect life, cruel death, and glorious resurrection of Jesus applied to the suffering sinner produces wonderful music. "Joy to the World" will become joy in his heart. He will not be able to stop the flow of music in his heart as he sings, "He lives, He lives! You ask me how I know He lives. He lives within my heart!" The supernatural grace of God within the heart of the sinner will always produce a wonderful song on the lips of the saint.

The third characteristic of the music of worship is that it is an instrument by which we acknowledge the ways of God. God's character is often discovered in the drama of human sorrow and pain. The ways of God lie far beyond the realm of man. However, His ways are often learned through the hurts of life. Worship becomes miraculous as misery is transformed into music in the theater of human experience.

When she was only six weeks old Fanny Crosby caught the cold that resulted in her blindness. What seemed to be human tragedy became divine triumph. God gave Fanny Crosby spiritual eyes to behold the glory of God. She wrote more than eight thousand sacred songs and hymns. One of the most popular of her hymns, "Blessed Assurance," expresses the triumph of God amidst the tragedy of a blind lady. She wrote, "Blessed Assurance, Jesus is mine! Oh, what a foretaste of glory divine! Heir of salvation, purchase of God, born of His Spirit, washed in His blood. This is my story, this is my song, praising my Savior all the day long." Fanny Crosby learned of the ways of God. Her music became an instrument to worship God in the midst of His sometimes mysterious but always marvelous ways.

Cautions Concerning Worship Through Music

Music is a vehicle. In itself it is not worship. It is rather a means by which the believer transports the deepest feelings of his heart to the heart of God. It is a method of expression of our love for God. The method, however, must never replace the essence of worship.

We need continually to remind ourselves of four basic cautions concerning the music of worship. First, we must guard ourselves against the familiarity of music. It is too easy to assemble with other Christians and sing the great songs of the faith. Quite often the song services of a church become a matter of tradition and ritual rather than of worship and praise. This is true not only among more traditional Christians but also among Christians who see themselves as non-traditional. Traditional Christians often find themselves simply mouthing words rather than praising God from the depths of their hearts, but the same is true also of those who sing the more modern, non-traditional choruses. They often become very "traditional" about their non-traditional songs. They sing Scripture choruses that have become familiar to them, but which have lost the essence of heartfelt worship. We must guard against the familiarity of music.

Second, true worship is rooted in the grace of God rather than in the performance of man. Therefore, we must be careful never to allow our music simply to be a showcase for our talent. The objective of true worship is the glory of God—never the greatness of our gifts. Music is an art that should be finely tuned to express the beauty and majesty of God.

The apostle Paul was an artist. His writings and teachings are those of a master. His epistles are among some of the great pieces of world literature. The great scholars of the church, such as Calvin and Luther, have been deeply affected by them. The great orators, such as Spurgeon, have studied them. World leaders still quote them. Yet Paul said, "My message and my preaching were not in persuasive words of wisdom, but in demonstration of the Spirit and of power, that your faith should not rest on the wisdom of men, but on the power of God" (1 Cor. 2:4-5). In other words, the artistic abilities of Paul were not to draw attention to the artist. They were to bring men and women to a personal knowledge of the power and glory of God.

Music that produces worship will be participatory in nature. True worship has no room for a spectating heart; the home of worship is in the participating heart. Worship cannot sit in the grandstands of the church watching the performance of the more talented. True worship flows from the heart that has been graced by God and cries out, "I must sing unto You for my heart is full. You, O God, have filled me with a knowledge of Your love. And You alone must I worship." True worship does not perform for others. It only participates in the grace and love of God.

The third caution concerning music is in regard to cultural misunderstanding. The one source of Christian unity should be the worship of Jesus Christ. Yet many times the music in our worship becomes a point of contention and division among Christians. Because I travel internationally, often I must adjust to new cultural forms of worship. That can sometimes be difficult. I think that my favorite place of worship is the nation of Romania. My personality and cultural upbringing seem to fit there. I love the poetry readings, the orchestras, and the congregational singing of the great hymns among Romanian Christians. I remember my first trip to India, however. Christian worship there was much less emotional. It took me a while to learn to enjoy it, for I was not used to the chanting and the more laid-back approach to worshiping God. Yet the worship was just as genuine as that in Romanina.

Later, I traveled into the bush in Africa. The form of worship was completely different among those people. There was plenty of emotion—much more than I was used to experiencing. Yet the people were worshiping God in spirit and in truth in all three places. They had three completely different expressions of music in their worship. But the essence of worship was the same. It was only the cultural personalities that differed.

I have discovered that Christians in the western world are often divided over the method of worship rather than the essence of worship. It is important for us to recognize our cultural and personality differences. We may feel more comfortable worshiping with those who sing only hymns. Or we may prefer to worship through the singing of Scripture choruses. Some participate more fully in an emotional expression of music. Others truly worship with a subdued, quiet spirit. But we must never forget that the end of true worship is not the method. The objective of true worship is the glory of Jesus. Therefore, let each of us worship Him in the method that fits our cultural personality. But let us not allow that personality to divide an evangelical community that holds fast to the glory of Jesus and the authority of the Scriptures.

Finally, music must never replace the priority of the Scriptures in worship. A renewal of worship is taking place in much of the evangelical community today. Many Christians are rediscovering the beauty of music in worship, and this is a tremendous development. We must be careful, however, to remember that music is a vehicle which transports a response to the revelation of God in the heart. It takes that response to the throne of heaven. There can be no response without the revelation of God. Buddhists, Muslims, Hindus, and Animists all sing, chant, and dance. But Christianity is not just another great world religion. It is the revelation of God to man through the person of Jesus, who is the "radiance of His glory and the exact representation of His nature" (Heb. 1:3).

Therefore, preaching of the word of God must never be replaced by the singing of the saints. In fact, many of the great hymns were written by preachers such as Luther, Wesley, Heber, and Perronet. Their music was a response to the God revealed to them in the Scriptures. There must be a balance in our worship between God's revelation and the heart's response to that revelation. Such worship will be not only music in the heart but also music in heaven.

NOTE

1. James McClelland, *The Stories Behind Great Hymns* (Belfast: Ambassador, 1985), pp. 122-23.

If I bow before Him in my inner chamber, then I am in contact with the eternal, unchanging power of God. . . . Oh, if we would only take time for the inner chamber so that we might experience in full reality the presence of this Almighty Jesus! What a blessedness would be ours through faith! An unbroken fellowship with an Omnipresent and Almighty Lord.

Andrew Murray,
The Prayer Life

Glory in His holy name; Let the heart of those who seek the Lord be glad. Seek the Lord and His strength; Seek His face continually.

Psalm 105:3-4

9
Prayer and Worship

One of the greatest lies foisted upon the modern church is that worship can only take place between 11:00 and 12:00 on Sunday mornings. Much of the church seems to think that true worship transpires only behind stained glass windows in beautifully decorated buildings. However, the beauty of biblical worship is that it knows nothing of time and space limitations. The place to worship Jesus Christ is only as far away as the inner chamber of the heart.

The chamber of prayer is capable of bringing the child of God directly to the throne of God. The Christian may find himself worshiping Jesus in a beautiful church sanctuary or in a lonely hospital room. He can worship in a modern office complex or in the solitude of his own home. The worship of God is only a prayer away.

Much that has been discussed in this book will be practically worked out in the prayer life of the believer. I first learned to worship in the school of prayer. The entire purpose of prayer is to lead God's people to the worship of Jesus Christ. When Jesus taught His disciples to pray, He opened and closed the door of prayer with the focus upon God. The door was opened with the petition, "Our Father who art in heaven, Hallowed be Thy name" (Matt. 6:9). He then closed the door of prayer with the ascription, "For Thine is the kingdom, and the power, and the glory, forever. Amen" (Matt. 6:13). The entire aim of prayer, according to Jesus, was the recognition that all of the kingdom, and all of the power, and all of the glory belonged only to God; the true goal of prayer is worship.

Jesus not only taught the disciples to acknowledge God's glory in prayer, but His own prayer life was an example of seeking the glory of God as well. The greatest biblical record of the intercessory prayer life of Jesus is His high priestly prayer. In John 17, He prays for His disciples and those who would come to a knowledge of God through their witness.

One word seems to consume the thoughts of Jesus as He prays. It is the word *glory*. In verse 5, Jesus prays for the glorification of God, crying out, "And now, glorify Thou Me together with Thyself, Father, with the glory which I had with Thee before the world was." Then He prays for the specific needs of the disciples. But He asks the Father to meet all of those needs for one purpose: "That they may all be one; even as Thou, Father, art in Me, and I in Thee, that they also may be in Us, that the world may believe that Thou didst send me" (v. 21). In the beginning of the conclusion of the prayer, Jesus expresses His desire that "they also, whom Thou hast given Me, be with Me where I am, in order that they may behold My glory, which Thou hast given Me" (v. 24).

My entire prayer life has been radically changed by understanding and practicing this principle of prayer. The deepest man of prayer I have ever met is a medical doctor in Romania. We have become the best of friends. Much of that friendship was brought into being through our prayer together. There is nothing that will bring a deeper fellowship of friends than the true worship of Jesus Christ.

When I first met this friend, he was interpreting for me as I preached evangelistic crusades. As we traveled together throughout Romania, we prayed. Most of his time of prayer was spent in worship. And when he did pray for the crusade or for other individuals, it was ultimately for the glory of God that he prayed. I have never been so challenged in all of my life about the true nature of prayer. I ceased praying for multitudes to come to Christ so that I could feel that we were accomplishing a part of the task of world evangelization. Instead, I began praying for people to come to Christ solely for the glory of God. I finally began to realize that the ultimate purpose of world evangelization rests solely in the glory of God.

Since I began to pray in such a manner, my entire ministry has been completely transformed. We have seen more people come to Christ than ever in our ministry. But more importantly, my motivation has been changed. I've begun to understand that the purpose of prayer is not to build my ministry or my own little empire. The purpose of prayer is to bring me to a genuine understanding that the kingdom, the power, and the glory belong only to Him. It is when I really understand that principle that I find myself worshiping Jesus.

Quite often after leading a seminar on prayer, I am approached by Christian leaders who express frustration about their prayer lives. They speak of dryness in prayer or a sense of simply "going through the motions" of prayer. The question people most often ask me is, "How can I know the joy of prayer?" The answer to that question is simply, "Joy in prayer is the fruit of the worship of Jesus Christ."

Many Christians are like the American boxer who trained for years to make the Olympic team. He worked, sweated, and suffered pain all for one goal—the glory of the Olympics. Yet after reaching the city of the Olympics, he missed the bus to his fight. He was so close to experiencing the Olympic glory, but he left empty-handed without even having come near it.

Many of us know there is a battle for the minds and hearts of men and women. We know that the arena for the battle is the place of prayer. It is in that place that God's glory dwells. However, some of us never get on the bus. We neglect the life of prayer, and consequently we miss the glory of God. Others catch the wrong bus and end up in the wrong place. We end up on a street called "self-glory." However, the address of true prayer is "the worship and glory of Jesus Christ."

NATURE OF PRAYER THAT RESULTS IN WORSHIP

Prayer that results in the true worship of Jesus has three basic characteristics. There must first be a total abandonment of the self-life. When Jesus called His disciples, He required them to abandon two things that could have kept them from a true knowledge of Himself. He said that each disciple must "deny himself" and "lose his life." It is the self-life that keeps us from a knowledge of the glory of the Christ-life. Therefore, we must learn to die to the self-life.

Prayer that originates in and is motivated by the self-life will only satisfy our ego needs and will never produce the glory of Jesus. The self-life always cries, "I want. . . . I think. . . . I desire." But the life of Christ in us prays, "Not my will, but Thy will be done." That kind of praying is powerful. It has as its chief end the glory and worship of God.

One of the most powerful men of prayer in the Christian church was George Mueller. He housed, clothed, and fed thousands of orphans solely through prayer. He provided financial support to the ministry of Hudson Taylor through the means of prayer. Mueller once stated that he believed that God had given him more than thirty thousand souls in answer to prayer. Mueller's principles of prayer were very specific. He wrote:

> There are five conditions [of prayer] which I always endeavor to fulfill, in observing which I have the assurance of answer to prayer:
>
> 1. "I have not the least doubt because I am assured that it is the Lord's will to save them, for He willeth that all men should be saved and come to a knowledge of the truth" (1 Tim. 2:4). . . .

2. "I have never pleaded for their salvation in my own name, but in the blessed name of my precious Lord Jesus, and on His merits alone (John 1:14).
3. "I always firmly believed in the willingness of God to hear my prayers (Mark 11:24).
4. "I am not conscious of having yielded to any sin, for 'if I regard iniquity in my heart, the Lord will not hear me' when I call (Ps. 66:18).
5. "I have persevered in believing prayer for more than fifty-two years for some, and shall continue till the answer comes: 'Shall not God avenge his own elect which cry day and night unto him' " (Luke 18:7).[1]

The secret to the prayer life of Mr. Mueller shines forth as a golden ray of sunlight. He prayed from the heart of Jesus to the glory of Jesus. His praying, from beginning to ending, was rooted in the life of Christ. His principles of effective praying had no seeds of self-motivation or self-glory. He planted his prayer life in Christ alone.

The second characteristic of prayer that produces worship is total surrender of one's heart to God. The heart that finds its supreme satisfaction in God experiences the depths of the love of Jesus Christ. A heart that is undivided in its loyalty becomes a worshiping heart. There must be a single-mindedness in our prayer lives if we are truly to worship God. We must desire only a knowledge of Him. Thomas Goodwin said, "I have known men who came to God for nothing else but just to come to Him, they so loved Him. They scorned to soil Him and themselves with any other errand than just purely to be alone with Him in His presence."[2]

When we thirst after a knowledge of God, we will find Him. All through the day we will long for special moments of aloneness. In those precious moments we will come into His presence. Our hearts belong to Him. We will want to be with Him, love Him, and worship Him. There will be a freshness in our love for Him when our hearts belong completely to Him.

Finally, we will have the high praises of God on our lips when we come to the inner chamber of prayer. And praise will be translated into worship. Something wonderful occurs when we praise God. Praise is the acknowledgment of the moral and spiritual attributes of God. When we begin to acknowledge Him for who He is, He comes to dwell in these praises. Imagine that. The eternal, omnipotent God actually lives in the heart that recognizes Him and the nature of His glory.

When the inner person beholds God, worship bursts forth in the heart just as the morning sunrise brings the glory of a new day. Sometimes the splendor of God will become so beautiful that we will be overwhelmed with His majesty. We will understand why Charles Wesley wrote, "O, for a thousand tongues to sing of the glory of my King." His beauty and majesty are so great that the highest praises are impossible for a mortal tongue to express. He is far beyond our highest comprehension and yet He is closer than our dearest friend. As we clothe ourselves with the high praise of God, we will discover that our garments of praise have become a wardrobe of worship.

PRACTICAL PRINCIPLES OF WORSHIP

The goal of all prayer is the true worship of Jesus Christ. Therefore, we must be very careful when we approach our times of prayer. Worship is the greatest journey upon which we can embark in life. We must know that we are fully prepared for the greatest adventure of our lives. There is nothing in life we will ever do that is more significant than worship. We were created with the capacity to know, love, and worship Him. And we are commanded to love Him with all our hearts. Worship is no small undertaking. It is so great that it engulfs the very meaning and purpose of our lives.

I have been careful to state that the essence of worship is not in our methods. But at this point I feel it is important to state some principles that will prevent distractions from interrupting our worship. These principles in themselves will not necessarily produce a heart of worship. But they will assist an already worshiping heart toward regularity and consistency in worship.

Principle 1: Solitude. We need a time and place in which we can meet alone with God. Genuine love breaks the barriers of superficiality. Love is deep. My wife and I have grown in our love relationship over the past twenty-one years. When we were first married I thought that I could never love a human as much as I loved her. But I discovered that that was not true. I love her more now than I did then. I have watched others whose love relationships have fallen apart. I have asked myself what the difference is between the two types of love relationships—those which last and those which fall apart. I have drawn one major conclusion: The love between my wife and me has grown because we have committed ourselves to times of intimate communication. We plan time each week to be alone and to share our deepest feelings. We take special time to be with each other to discover one another's dreams and goals.

The same principle applies to our relationship with God. We must plan time to be alone with Him and to learn what is on His heart. And we must share with Him the deep things on our hearts. Our love relationship with God must never become superficial. We need to schedule times of solitude with Him.

Principle 2: Meditation. Solitude brings us to the place of worship, but meditation introduces us to the Person we worship. Meditation is at the very heart of Christian worship. It is much more than some sort of mystical approach to God. It places our focus on the person of Christ and allows His divine attributes and moral character to transform our inner being. David was a man after God's own heart, and he didn't live as a monk, alienated from society. His life was productive and useful. Yet he speaks of meditating on the law of God day and night. He knew how to be still and acknowledge God as God.

The term *meditation* frightens many western Christians because of its usage among the eastern religions. However, biblical meditation is entirely different from Eastern mysticism. Meditation for the Christian is not emptying his mind of all his thought. It is just the opposite. It is filling his mind with the One who is altogether pure, lovely, and honorable.

Christian meditation focuses on the Word of God. From Genesis to Revelation, the Scriptures point us to Jesus. In them, we are able to see the marvelous nature of Jesus. In Genesis He is *in* the beginning, but in Revelation He *is* the beginning and the end—the Alpha and Omega. In Daniel He is the Ancient of Days, and in Colossians He is the firstborn of all creation. In John He is the only begotten Son of God, and in Hebrews He is the radiance of God's glory and the exact representation of His nature. So much of His glory and so many of His attributes are described in the Bible. Every day we should find ourselves in some lonely spot at a specified time with our Bibles open and our hearts quiet. We will then gain true appreciation for the Savior.

Principle 3: Adoration. The natural response to the fresh insight of the nature and character of Christ we gain will be adoration. As our hearts and minds focus on Jesus, a deep sense of love will begin to flow from the innermost part of our lives. We will worship Jesus Christ. It is to this end that all prayer should be directed. Many Christians have not experienced the joy of prayer because they have never really understood the ultimate objective of prayer.

The "asking," "seeking," and "knocking" of prayer is not a form of self-indulgence. We ask because we are needy children. We seek Him because He is everything we need. We knock because we desire to enter into a sweet fellowship and daily walk with Him. Through that kind of prayer we will come to know God as the Father who is perfect in His goodness. The true objective of prayer is the adoration of God through His Son, Jesus. Find a quiet place on a regular basis and open the Book. Behold the Lamb of God. Fall on your face and worship Him.

NOTES

1. Andrew Murray, *The Prayer Life* (Chicago: Moody), pp. 123-24.
2. J. Oswald Chambers, *Prayer Power Unlimited*, Billy Graham Crusade edition (Chicago: Moody, 1977), p. 7.

Above all, keep much in the presence of God. Never see the face of man till you have seen His face, who is our life—our all.

Robert Murray M'Cheyne, in *The Life of Robert Murray M'Cheyne*

And day by day continuing with one mind in the temple, and breaking bread from house to house, they were taking their meals together with gladness and sincerity of heart, praising God, and having favor with all the people. And the Lord was adding to their number day by day those who were being saved.

Acts 2:46-47

10
Witness and Worship

The earthly life of Jesus was given to one great purpose —the redemption of mankind. His every action was designed to bring men and women into a proper relationship with the Father. However, He knew that all humanity must experience forgiveness in order to enter into such a relationship. Consequently, He knew that He must die. Someone would have to accept the punishment for the sins of the world, and He was sent for that purpose.

He kept telling the disciples that there was one reason for His life: He was born to die. He had to go to Jerusalem and suffer on a cruel Roman cross. He was the Lamb of God, who would take away the sins of the world. He offered His life as a sacrifice for the sins of all people of all times.

The day finally came that He fulfilled His life's ultimate purpose. He hung on the cross and cried, "It is finished." He had accomplished the task to which He had been called. However, the Father in heaven did not allow the Son to suffer defeat by the wicked forces of the universe. He raised His Son from the dead and exalted Him above everything in existence. He gave Him a name that is above all names.

Before Jesus ascended to the right hand of the Father, He appeared to His disciples. He gave them a commission to go into the whole world and preach this good news: every person, no matter how sinful, can now be reconciled to his holy, pure Creator because of the blood that was shed on that Roman cross outside of Jerusalem. The disciples were to proclaim Him. He was the good news. They were to teach men and women to obey all that He had taught them. They were to proclaim His sinless life, His atoning death, and the power of His resurrection.

But Jesus told His disciples to tarry in Jerusalem before they began their mission. Why did Jesus tell them to wait? The world was such a needy place. Why did He not want them *immediately* to be about the task of world evangelization?

The answer was simple. They needed to be "clothed with power from on high" (Luke 24:49). Consequently, the New Testament church did not begin with its focus outward, but with the hearts of the believers looking upward. The New Testament church began in a prayer meeting. Jesus laid the foundation of the church by turning the hearts of the disciples heavenward. It is interesting to note the pattern that develops throughout the book of Acts. The church prays, and then it proclaims the good news of God's salvation to man.

It is in prayer that the church finds its power to proclaim the forgiveness of Jesus. The purpose of prayer is to worship Jesus Christ. In the worship experience we find the power to witness of His love and of His power to save those who believe in Him. The ultimate purpose of world evangelization is to fill the whole earth with His glory. The effective witness of Jesus is the one who has the glory of God written on the tablet of his heart.

The purpose of telling others about Jesus is primarily for the glory of God. Many have become discouraged and have ceased witnessing because of an inadequate understanding of the purpose of witnessing. If I were to ask most evangelical Christians why we should tell others the gospel, I would probably receive a variety of responses. Some would say, "People are dying and going to hell. They need to be saved." That's true, but it is an inadequate answer for three basic reasons. First, it places the focus of salvation on the needs of man. Second, it places a great burden on the one witnessing for Christ rather than on the Holy Spirit. The work of salvation is a work of God's grace that is produced by the Holy Spirit. It is the responsibility of the Christian to be obedient in sharing his faith. It is the responsibility of the Holy Spirit to draw people to the Savior. Third, escape from hell is a secondary benefit of salvation. The primary benefit is that men and women are brought into a proper relationship with God, which brings glory to God.

When I came to this understanding, my entire perspective on witnessing was transformed. I ceased telling others of Christ out of a sense of guilt. I began sharing Christ as a result of my love and worship of Him. I wanted others to know Him because of how great and majestic He is. My witnessing began to result from the overflow of my worship.

The great heroes of the faith have been men and women who were consumed with the glory of God. Their every action was motivated by the majesty and glory of God. This motivation has inspired the great preachers of every generation. It has ignited the flames of missionary movements and world evangelization.

Those who have most impacted my life and my philosophy of ministry have not necessarily been the most well-known Christians. They have been the ones who have given their lives to worshiping the Savior and making His worthiness known to all people. They will probably never be known throughout the Christian community, but their worship is well-known in heaven.

While ministering in India I met a young Indian who was ministering among the tribal peoples in the state of Gujarat. He probably will never speak at any large conferences. His name will probably never be a household word in the Christian community. This young man lives among the tribal peoples at the risk of contracting deadly diseases. Hundreds of people have died recently as a result of a cholera epidemic. He works with the Methodist church in the Gujarat, sponsoring medical clinics for needy people. He helps them plant and harvest their crops. He helps to educate them, he teaches them the Bible, and he has brought a number of them to Jesus.

What has motivated a young Indian Christian to risk deadly disease and rejection, chosing to live away from his peers? His salary is low. There is no fame in his work. He lives in uncomfortable surroundings. He is motivated by the same thing that motivated Judson, Carey, and Brainard. They have seen the glory of the Savior in such a way that their entire lives have been dedicated to telling others about Him. They haven't shared Christ in order to build their own ministries or kingdoms. The cry of their hearts has been, "For Thine is the kingdom, and the power, and the glory, forever. Amen" (Matt. 6:13).

WORSHIP PRODUCES PURITY AND POWER

There are two great needs in the life of a Christian who is to be an effective witness of Christ: purity of character and power. The platform from which a person shares Christ with others is purity of character. It is not the dynamic of our gifts and abilities that causes people to really listen to us. It is what we are on the inside.

The church faces a great character crisis in this generation. I am convinced that the cause of the crisis is our failure truly to worship Jesus Christ. We have made worship a matter of form and method, rather than really giving Jesus the glory that is due His name. Several years ago God gave me a perspective on temptation. At the time, my approach to temptation was simple. There were certain sins that were taboo for a Christian minister, so I would never do any of those things. Sins such as immorality would destroy my family. Therefore, I would attempt to stay away from immoral situations. Other sins would damage my body. Therefore, I refrained from those things. I basically liked myself, and I wanted to live as long as possible.

There was, however, a basic problem with this approach to temptation. It approached victory over sin from a negative perspective, and consequently, it produced legalism. Legalism can help a person keep the outward forms of God's law. But it does nothing to build a person's inward character. The non-Christian world needs to see much more in the Christian than abstinence from smoking, drinking, or involving himself in immoral affairs. The world needs also to see the inward beauty of the character of the Christian.

When God began to work in my heart in this matter, I experienced some tremendous changes of attitude and character. My attitude about sin became one that was built on a positive relationship with Christ rather than a negative fear of what might happen to my ministry, my family, or myself. I am not speaking of "the power of positive thinking." I am speaking of the power of worshiping the lovely Lamb of God. When I see Him in all of His glory, I want to do nothing that would discredit Him. I flee immorality, not just for my benefit, but for His name's sake. I refrain from certain activities not only because they will harm me, but primarily because I want to glorify God with my body. He is worthy of being glorified in my family, ministry, and personal life.

The yearning for the glory of God produces a positive kind of Christianity. It produces character in the believer that enables him to share Christ in a world that is wrecked by sin. Without Christlike character our words will fall on deaf ears. In fact, much of the time they will produce negative results rather than positive ones.

The worship of Jesus Christ will not only produce inner character in the life of the Christian, but it will also give him power to share his faith. There is a certain amount of confidence in witnessing that comes through consistency in our deeds and words. But there is an even greater enduement of power that comes from the worship of Jesus Christ.

Two of the New Testament apostles, Peter and John, had an extraordinary power to share Christ during the early days of the church. It seemed as though everywhere they went and everything they touched turned into an opportunity to witness of Jesus. They were walking to a prayer meeting and ended up shaking the city of Jerusalem for the glory of God. They accomplished more for Christ accidentally than most Christians today accomplish intentionally.

In the first few chapters of Acts we find Peter speaking with great confidence about Christ. Thousands are converted. A lame man is healed. Peter and John are arrested and threatened. Then an interesting observation is made about them: "Now as they observed the confidence of Peter and John, and understood that they were uneducated and untrained men, they were marveling, and began to recognize them as having been with Jesus" (Acts 4:13). The secret of their power and confidence to proclaim Christ was not in their great oratorical skills. Nor was it in their education. They had been with Jesus! The secret to the great courage and boldness of the apostles was simply the worship of Jesus Christ.

OVERCOMING OBSTACLES TO WITNESSING

We live in a generation that has more information about how to witness than perhaps any other generation since the time of Christ. We have the inverse of Peter and John. There seem to be many educated and trained witnesses for Christ, but few who have the power and courage to share Him with others. Three major obstacles in the lives of Christians will hinder their ability to tell others about Jesus. The worship of Jesus Christ enables the believer to overcome these obstacles.

Obstacle 1: A fearful spirit. The greatest single hindrance to witnessing is fear. We fear what others will think. We fear failure. We fear making fools of ourselves. We fear rejection. All of these fears create a powerful force to prevent us from telling others about Jesus. I have shared Christ with atheists, Hindus, Muslims, communists, animists, humanists, and nominal Christians. I have had to deal with almost every ideology imaginable. Yet the greatest hindrance to my witness has not been opposing ideologies. The greatest barrier has been my own fear. I must confess that I deal with fear almost every time I share Christ with others.

The antithesis of fear is love. Fear points to self, while love points to others. Fear is negative, but love is positive. Fear makes us insecure, but love secures our lives to the Rock that is immovable. "Perfect love casts out fear" (1 John 4:18).

Perfect love is found at the throne of God. When we come before His throne, we encounter the One who is love. Peter and John were made courageous for Christ because they had worshiped Him, their Savior. Years later John wrote, "God is love" (1 John 4:8). It is only as we worship Jesus that we are engulfed in His love. As we are filled with His love, fear seems to disappear. Our security is in Him. When we find our acceptance in Him, all fear must flee. Fear cannot dwell in the heart of the one who worships Jesus Christ. The fearful heart becomes a courageous heart.

Obstacle 2: A frustrated spirit. Many opportunities to share the gospel are lost because of unresolved conflicts within the heart of the believer. Jesus told His disciples not to be fearful or troubled in their hearts. He warned them of difficulties that they would have to face in the world.

It is a fact of life that every Christian will face difficult situations. However, if we are to be witnesses for Christ we must first learn how to deal with difficulties in the Spirit of Christ. Many times it is the little problems that eat away the peace in our hearts. We find ourselves frustrated, and consequently we miss many opportunities to witness.

The solution to frustration is peace. Jesus said, "Peace I leave with you; My peace I give to you; not as the world gives, do I give you" (John 14:27). The peace of Jesus is a unique kind of peace. It is not controlled by outward circumstances. It travels beyond petty problems and great tribulations. It goes all the way to the depths of the human heart. Peace fills the heart of the one whose eyes are fixed on Jesus.

It is the worshiping heart that experiences the "peace that surpasses all comprehension" (Phil. 4:7).

The door of difficulty often leads to the street of opportunity. It is on that street that we discover many opportunities to share Christ. However, the "difficult door" can only be opened with a key called "peace." That key is found in the throne room of God. As we worship Jesus Christ, our hearts are flooded with beautiful peace.

Several years ago I spoke at a Christian university about the necessity of spiritual awakening in this generation. I had many precious times of worship during the week. The more I worshiped Jesus Christ, the more I felt a great burden to tell others about Him. I asked God for an opportunity to tell someone of His great love.

When I boarded the plane to fly home, I was seated next to a lady with a screaming baby. As the plane took off, the baby screamed louder and louder. As the baby screamed, the mother became very frustrated. Tension began to mount in my heart. I thought, "Oh, no. I'm going to have to listen to this screaming baby for the entire trip."

As I looked at the situation, peace fled from my heart. But then the Holy Spirit began to convict me of my wrong attitude. He turned my focus to Jesus. I began to silently worship Him. The Spirit of God brought to my remembrance that Jesus is the King who became a Servant. I was faced with this question: What would Jesus do if He were here?

I realized that Jesus would serve that lady. I asked her if I could play with the baby. Immediately she said, "Please do." I made funny faces, acted silly, and talked baby talk. I laughed as I thought to myself, "Is this what it means to be filled with the Holy Spirit?"

Finally the baby calmed down and fell asleep. The lady thanked me for assisting her and then began to ask me many questions. I shared Christ with her. As I was speaking to her she began to weep. Her husband was a medical doctor, and neither of them were Christians. Her mother-in-law had become a Christian just a few weeks prior to our meeting. The mother-in-law told her son and daughter-in-law about Jesus. However, because she was a new Christian she felt inadequate. She told them, "I'm going to pray that God will send someone to you to explain His salvation more fully."

There I sat on that airplane as an answer to that mother's prayer. Yet I could have missed the opportunity. The choice was mine. I could have endured a plane ride next to a screaming baby. Or I could worship Jesus and unlock the door of difficulty with the key of peace.

Each of us faces that same choice every day. I am convinced that we must learn to worship Jesus if we are to win a world that lives on a street filled with tribulation to Christ.

Obstacle 3: A negative spirit. If a person does not know how to deal with frustrations, he may develop a negative outlook on life. Unfortunately, many Christians are in this category.

The gospel is good news. When we know, love, and worship the Savior, our whole perspective on life changes. We develop a positive spirit and attitude. There is joy in the rule of God in the heart of man. That joy is the overflow of the heart that has worshiped Jesus. It is in worship that we discover the purpose of God. It is God's intent that the whole earth be filled with His glory. There is righteousness, peace, and joy where the glory of God dwells.

The heart that has worshiped Jesus will be committed to world evangelization. He is not only worthy of our worship; He is worthy of the worship of men and women of every national, racial, ethnic, and tribal origin. Therefore, the bottom line of true worship is world evangelization. This is an exciting generation in which to live. The world has been corrupted by the rebellious nature of man. There is great human suffering on every continent. But in the midst of wars, famine, pollution, and population explosion, there stands a Savior. He alone can bring peace to the hurting heart and righteousness and justice to the nations. The door of difficulty can be opened with the key of peace. There are enormous opportunities to bring our world to Jesus. However, we must first go to the throne room. We must worship the worthy One. The key to world evangelization will be found at the feet of Jesus. Let us bow before Him. Then let us walk into a world that is hurting and proclaim the power and love of the One who is worthy of the worship of all humanity.

Moody Press, a ministry of the Moody Bible Institute, is designed for education, evangelization, and edification. If we may assist you in knowing more about Christ and the Christian life, please write us without obligation: Moody Press, c/o MLM, Chicago, Illinois 60610.